ABCDE
FGHIJK
LMNOP
QRSTUV
WXYZ

A
dictionary
of political
analysis

Geoffrey K. Roberts, Ph.D.

St. Martin's Press
New York

Published in the United States of America in 1971
by St. Martin's Press, Inc.
175 Fifth Avenue, New York 10010

Printed in Great Britain

Dedicated
To My
Parents

5-22-72 Book, 7.16

Contents

Acknowledgements

I wish to thank my colleagues in the Department of Social Sciences at Loughborough University who have helped me with valuable suggestions concerning particular entries in this dictionary, and especially Albert Cherns, John Frears and William Jenkins who read, and commented on, drafts of several of the entries. Responsibility for the contents, of course, remains with the author. I am also grateful to my wife, Mechthild, and to Jennifer Mortimer, for assistance with the typing and collation of the entries, and to my students at Loughborough who stimulated the whole enterprise in various ways.

Geoffrey K. Roberts

Introduction

Science is the description, classification and analysis of the nature of material and abstract things, and the understanding of their relationships. Every branch of science relies on the naming of these things and their properties and relationships, to enable the scientist both to recall their properties and attributes to himself at some future time, and to communicate information about them to other people, particularly to other scientists. But to be of such use, the words used as 'names' to denote objects of scientific attention must have specific and very precise reference values. Imprecision of definition leads to ambiguity of communication, and therefore scientific vocabularies consist of, or aim to consist of, specialised and well defined terms with denotations of the greatest precision obtainable. These terms may refer to objects such as uranium, electrons or cumulo-nimbus cloud, qualities like electrical conductivity or elasticity, units of measurement such as the volt, the micron or absolute zero, phenomena such as gravity, processes such as photosynthesis or nuclear fission, or concepts such as infinity or equilibrium. Whatever they are, they carry with them a quality of 'agreed exactitude', that is to say, two chemists, or astronomers or physicists will, to a very great degree, when using the same word be referring to the same object or process.

Of course, controversies exist concerning the exact nature or properties of certain phenomena or objects even in those disciplines most concerned with precision of definition, especially when new terms are introduced, or comparatively vague phenomena—such as 'life', 'intelligence' or 'the universe'—are concerned. Nor does agreement over definition preclude controversy over causation (the question of the origin of the moon, or the arguments over the 'steady state' or 'expansion' of the universe, are examples). But it is not necessary for natural scientists to set out new definitions, or even to consult dictionaries, to describe and analyse most of the phenomena with which they are concerned. Chemists agree on what H_2O refers to, and on what to call 'water'; the biologist recognises the term 'gene' as used by his colleagues, even if he has never had the opportunity of discussing the definition with them. Common and accepted definitions are the rule in the natural and physical sciences.

Yet in the social sciences, and in the realm of political science in particular, arguments over naming and definition still occupy much of the undergraduate's education, the research output of postgraduates, the cogitations of the professors, the pages of the learned journals, and the sessions of professional conferences. Discussions over the meaning of the word 'nation', over whether Rhodesia is a 'state', or whether 'natural law' is 'law', over the shades of meaning that can be read in (or into) Machiavelli's concept of *fortuna*—these have been the staple diet of most British scholars in political studies, despite the warning of Weldon against 'the primitive and generally unquestioned belief that words, and especially the words which normally occur in discussions about politics such as "State", "Citizen", "Law", and "Liberty", have intrinsic or essential meanings which it is the aim of political philosophers to discover and explain',[1] and the clear statement of Barbara Wootton that 'the meaning of terms is purely a matter of verbal convention'.[2]

As Humpty Dumpty so forcefully declared to Alice, words are signs to indicate whatever users wish them to indicate, though, of course, they may not do this very successfully or efficiently. In this way they are no different from a code, except that in the case of ordinary language the whole of the literate population has been taught the meanings of many of the code-words. In the case of a scientific or technical vocabulary, the code is—or should be—

1. T. D. Weldon, *The Vocabulary of Politics*, Penguin, 1953, pp. 11–12.
2. Barbara Wootton, 'Terminology in the social sciences', *International Social Science Journal* ii, no. 1, 1950, 47.

comprehensible to the specialised audience to which it is addressed. Although one tends to accept the language learned in childhood, or in studying a discipline, and to use it out of tradition or habit, the process in logic is no different from two people, on being faced with an object, agreeing that 'from now on, when we wish to refer to this object, or this class of objects, or to other objects similar in respect of this and that relevant quality, let us call them X'—and this process being repeated for all the objects, attitudes, phenomena, etc., with which a population is concerned. Nor is there any objection, in logic, to some people agreeing to call that same object Y, though if the two sets of people wish to communicate about the object concerned, their communication will not be effective until they have made clear to each other that X and Y in fact refer to the same thing.

Thus the test involved in such a question as 'is Hungary—a "people's democracy"—*really* a democracy?' is not what the essential or 'true' meaning of democracy is, and how closely Hungary's political system matches this meaning, but whether political scientists find it useful to define 'democracy' by using testable attributes that include, or exclude, the case of Hungary. This is just the same process whereby biologists have found it more useful to define a whale as a mammal rather than as a fish, despite frequent attribution of the whale to the class 'fish' by the lay public. Further, the argument between western and Communist users of the word 'democracy' is not an argument about how well some specified cases match an agreed set of criteria involved in 'democracy' as a concept, but an example of two (or more) completely differing definitions of the word 'democracy'. Even should there be agreement on a definition in this example, the argument would not end, but would reveal itself for what it is, an argument about preferences rather than empirical facts. Hence, though it might still be heresy to say so, if a word like 'democracy' causes problems in the discourse of political scientists on account of its lack of an 'agreed exactitude' and its ambiguities arising from its usages in non-scientific contexts, and if it cannot in any case be given a precise, operational definition, then may it not be advisable to abandon it to the slogan writers, philosophers and Sunday political journalists to play with? A more precise word can be found instead, or invented.

It may justly be argued that the phenomena of the natural and physical sciences are easier to define with precision than are the phenomena of the social sciences, since the behaviour of things physical is more regular than the behaviour of things human and social, particularly the behaviour of 'political man'. Certainly many of the concepts, processes and institutions with which political scientists are concerned are of a high level of complexity. 'No science, however, has ever made much progress without the help of an exact technical vocabulary; nor can the social sciences hope to be an exception to this rule.'[1] Science involves a search for regularities and relationships; political science will only advance in its understanding of political life by seeking in it such regularities and relationships as may exist, by seizing on the important distinctions that separate two or more complex phenomena, by discovering the major factors that account for a complicated interaction. All men are different. All their societies and their politics are different. But similarities and regularities do exist. The discovery, analysis, and precise and unambiguous definition of these similarities are the important tasks confronting political scientists.

THE AIMS AND SCOPE OF THE DICTIONARY

Having, as it were, counselled such perfection, it must immediately be made clear that the author makes no claim that this dictionary has achieved it. It is a mirror of the present vocabulary of the discipline, not a proposal for a future technical word list from which all ambiguities and imprecisions have been removed. Thus terms which, while vague or possessed of multiple definitions, are part of the current vocabulary of the books and academic discourse of political science, are included and such vagueness or multiplicity is pointed out in the definition, though the author has not felt disbarred from stating preferences for particular usages.

Excluded from the entries, in general, are personal names, events and places: the material *for* political study, rather than the means of studying politics. In all but a few cases, mainly where they are passing into more general use, 'culture specific' terms: British, American, Russian, classical, European, etc., have also been omitted, e.g. 'log-rolling', 'Fraktion' and 'democratic centralism'.

Terms have been included generally if they belong to one of the following categories:

—terms employed in social science methodology of relevance to political analysis (e.g. axiom, conceptual framework, hypothesis, validation);
—the discipline of political science, its distinctive subject-matter,

1. Wootton, *ibid.*

subdivisions of the discipline, areas of overlap with other disciplines, and closely related special study areas (e.g. politics, government, political analysis, political geography, policy analysis);

—concepts and approaches used for classification and analysis in political science (e.g. content analysis, feedback, systems analysis);

—concepts, institutions and processes which comprise the subject-matter of political science (e.g. anomie, executive, majority, plebiscite, regime);

—forms of political organisation (e.g. aristocracy, theocracy),

—types of political community (e.g. colony, confederation, industrial society, metropolis);

—major political ideologies and belief-systems which have influenced political thinking (e.g. anarchy, Communism, Zionism).[1]

Within these groups, many terms will no doubt be discovered by any reader which will appear to be self-explanatory. No apologies are made on this account, since the range of terms is intended to be as comprehensive as possible within the boundaries set by the aims of the dictionary, and—as the author knows only too well from practical experience—what to one reader may be 'self-explanatory' to another may be completely novel. It is hoped that this dictionary will serve many uses, but among its audience will be a section of the growing number of students new to the study of politics, in the universities and the polytechnics. Since few of them will have touched on subjects involving many of these concepts in their sixth-form syllabuses, for them only a small proportion of the definitions will already be known.

Particularly, attention has been paid to groups of terms where meanings may often be confused, or which are only subtly distinguished, if distinguished at all, from each other, e.g. revolution, putsch, coup d'état, rebellion, civil war, civil disobedience; Marxism, Communism, socialism, anarchy, syndicalism; plebiscite, referendum; political theory, political philosophy, political thought.

For this reason also, as well as to allow readers to broaden their comprehension of a term by comparison or relation to other terms,

---

1. It should be noted that, throughout this work, the author defines ideology widely, to refer to any implicit or explicit set of fundamental values from which attitudes, opinions and actions derive (see IDEOLOGY; 'LADDER OF VALUES').

cross-references deliberately have been supplied as fully as possible. These refer either to a similar, but distinguishable, term (e.g. power and authority), or to terms which provide a wider context for the term defined (e.g. charisma and leadership), or to terms used in a definition which are separately defined elsewhere, though this only occurs where the use of the term in the definition is of particular importance. These are indicated by the symbol ☛. The symbol ☞ is used for words defined under an alternative term.

Some terms are used in two distinct senses, and here they have been differentiated by the letters (A), (B), followed by a brief subordinate term or phrase, e.g. CONVENTION (A): the institution, CONVENTION (B): procedural conventions.

It is not claimed that the selection of terms, nor the definitions, will meet with universal approval; it is maintained that warrant exists in the literature of political science for each definition given, though in many cases overlapping definitions have been amalgamated, or, where several distinct definitions exist, these have been mentioned and one selected as possibly being more useful than the others, and given more extended treatment here. Certainly the author would welcome any new candidates for inclusion in any revised edition that may appear.

A

Abdication

The act of formal relinquishment of high office. Though especially applicable to a monarch or emperor renouncing his throne (e.g. Edward VIII in 1936 in Britain, and the German Kaiser in 1918), the term can also be used to refer to the abandonment of any position of leadership.

Absolute majority

☞ MAJORITY

Absolutism

A form of rule in which the rulers claim absolute, or total, power by virtue of personal attributes, the authority or the nature of the laws they interpet and apply, religious authority, the recognition of some form of 'necessity', or similar reasons.

In order to maintain an absolutist form of rule, rulers must reject any external limitation on their powers, such as custom, precedent, rival interpretations of the laws (e.g. through judicial review), an autonomous constitution which stands above the laws of the ruler, or claims by other social organisations (e.g. the churches, trade unions), to possess degrees of power in their own spheres.

Totalitarian states and theocracies are both forms of absolutist rule.

☛ AUTOCRACY; JUDICIAL REVIEW; THEOCRACY;
TOTALITARIANISM

Abstention

Failure to exercise one's right to vote. The word implies some element of deliberate refusal, but as used more loosely of national and local elections, for instance, the number of abstentions is usually derived by subtracting the total number of votes cast, including spoilt votes, from the number of possible eligible votes. This may be expressed in percentage form as the 'rate of abstention'.

☛ APATHY

Access

The ability of a political actor—individual or group—to obtain the attention of political decision-makers to the communication of demands. It is thus a pre-condition of the exercise of political influence, though it is not a sufficient condition for its exercise.

Access varies according to the political resources available to the individual or group, the importance of the actor's interest area as perceived by decision-makers, and the structure of governmental institutions (e.g. prima facie it is easier to obtain access to some group of governmental decision-makers in a federal system, than in a unitary system, or in a system with strict separation of powers than in one with relatively unified powers).

A fuller treatment of problems of access may be found in D. Truman, *The Governmental Process*, New York, Knopf, 1951.

☛ GROUP BASIS OF POLITICS; POLITICAL RESOURCES

Action theory

Associated particularly with the works of Talcott Parsons, action theory attempts to identify a comprehensive set of concepts and typologies, and to arrange them into an explanatory system, which can be applied to the analysis of actions (defined as motivated behaviour) of individuals, and the systems they comprise. It is a type of systems analysis, but is also of considerable relevance to behaviourally oriented studies.

A 2

The components of a social act are: an actor and his motivations; the purpose envisaged by him for his action; the external situation in which the action is set; the rules or norms which constrain his action. The relationships between actors, social actions and the environment constitute a system. This system, set in a hierarchy of systems, possesses a set of shared values, norms, etc., which constitute its 'culture'. It is also an adaptive system, able to persist and to fulfil certain functional imperatives, including pattern maintenance (the preservation of the culture and the institutional elements of the system); goal attainment (coordinated actions to pursue changes in the relationships between elements of the system, or between the system and its environment, that would be 'preferable' in terms of the values of the culture of the system); adaptation (the ability of the system to obtain and use resources to control the relationships of elements of the system and to respond to stresses of the environment); integration (the maintenance of relations between elements of the system that are 'functional' or desirable in terms of the persistence of the system).

Systems tend to develop specialised subsystems to carry out these functions: pattern maintenance by the cultural and familial institutions of society; goal attainment by the polity; adaptation by the economy; integration by the subsystem of stratification and social control. These subsystems are involved in exchanges with each other and with the environment.

The main criticisms of action theory have centred around its ambiguities and the generality of its concepts, and the teleological assumptions it seems to accept. As a type of structural-functional explanation, it is also open to the criticisms made with regard to the 'functional imperatives' notions which such theories and models often include.

☞ ADAPTATION; BEHAVIOURAL APPROACH; GOAL ATTAINMENT; PATTERN MAINTENANCE; STRUCTURAL-FUNCTIONAL ANALYSIS; SYSTEMS ANALYSIS

Adaptation

Processes of adjustment or 'learning', in response to exchanges with the environment and to stress arising from internal and external sources, that enable a system (hence, in political analysis, a political system) to persist, and to improve its capabilities for coping with stress and responding to its environment. Stress arising from an increase in demands, for instance, may lead to the system adapting by developing an improvement in its capacities for converting demands to policies.

☞ ENVIRONMENT; RESPONSE; STRESS; SYSTEMS ANALYSIS

Administration

The activity concerned with the implementation of policies by the direction or management of the efforts of individuals and groups towards specified goals.

Thus in politics it is the function of the executive branch, the 'third power' of government, the legislature and judiciary being the other two. While administration may include activities of decision-making that amount, in effect, to the making of policy, the formal setting of priorities is usually carried out by the legislature, and while administration may involve quasi-judicial forms of arbitration, the formal processes of decision concerning breaches of the law are carried out by the judiciary.

The term may also be used to refer to a particular period in which a government is in power, e.g. the Attlee administration, or the Nixon administration.

☞ BUREAUCRACY; EXECUTIVE; GOVERNMENT (A): the institution; PUBLIC ADMINISTRATION; SEPARATION OF POWERS

Administrative law

Administrative law is the branch of the legal codes of a political community concerned with the regulation of the activities of the executive branch of government, the proper legal boundaries of such activities, and the remedies of persons or groups aggrieved by administrative action.

The sources and content of administrative law will vary from country to country, as will the juridical arrangements for handling cases. In particular, countries of continental Europe, in contrast to the British Commonwealth and the United States of America, have a much wider-ranging area of content for administrative law (including e.g. aspects of administrative relationships that would not be matters for the courts in Britain or the USA), and generally possess a separate system of administrative courts to handle cases involving administrative departments or agencies, whereas in Anglo-Saxon legal systems the normal civil courts deal with such cases.

Though the sources and the substance of administrative law overlap with those of constitutional law, the latter also deals with matters concerning the legislative and judicial branches of government, and with the political rights and duties of private citizens, as well as, in the case of federal states, with the relationship between the federal and the provincial units of government. Administrative law, while including aspects of constitutional law, also deals with matters (e.g. the negligence of administrators) that are equivalent to ordinary civil matters of e.g. tort, contract or criminal law.

☛ ADMINISTRATION; ADMINISTRATIVE TRIBUNAL; CONSTITUTIONAL LAW; EXECUTIVE; OMBUDSMAN

Administrative tribunal

Administrative tribunals are quasi-judicial bodies created by governments for the purpose of adjudicating on questions of fact and law which arise out of the administration of statutes passed by the legislature. Their powers and composition are usually stated in the sections of the statute with which they are involved. Membership is by no means confined to legally qualified persons; lay members and various types of expert are frequently included. They are thus an alternative to the ordinary courts, and usually present a speedier and simpler method for the settlement of disputes involving the administration of legislation. They should not, however, be confused with the administrative courts of certain continental legal systems.

Examples include: tribunals concerned with appeals against conscription into the armed forces, with disputes over taxation assessments, and with appeals against refusal to grant certain types of licence. In Britain the constitution and methods of working of tribunals are kept under review by the Council on Tribunals, set up in 1958, particularly with regard to their standards of judicial procedure.

Aggregation

The process of collating a range of associated demands on some subject, e.g. tax reform, changes in the electoral system, relations with a neighbouring state, the structure of secondary education, and converting them from a fairly imprecise and miscellaneous state into a coherent policy proposal. In terms of the political system, it is thus the method by which demand inputs are changed into forms suitable for processing by the political system before conversion into outputs, e.g. as legislation or decree.

Aggregation may be performed through the agency of, for example, political parties, interest groups, the bureaucracy, the media of mass communication, legislators, or by members of the governmental authorities.

☛ INPUT-OUTPUT ANALYSIS; ISSUES; SYSTEMS ANALYSIS

Alien

An inhabitant of a country who owes allegiance to a foreign state, or who is declared stateless. An alien is thus usually prohibited from exercising political rights possessed by the nationals of the country concerned, such as voting or standing as a candidate in elections. The laws regarding naturalisation of aliens vary from state to state, but usually they impose minimum periods of residence among other requirements.

☛ CITIZEN

Alienation

A state of psychological isolation from either parts of one's own personality, or from significant aspects of one's social existence. The term is used by Marx, for instance, to indicate the psychological separation of the worker's social personality from his personality in its productive aspect under conditions of capitalism, where 'labour' is treated as a factor of production rather than an expression of the human personality. When a person is placed in a strange social context, especially if this is against his will, he may refuse (consciously or unconsciously) to involve himself psychologically in that society, even though his actions, forced and unforced, conform to the requirements of that society. This is also 'alienation'. Examples of the latter form of alienation were found in the cases of concentration camp victims in the Second World War.

Alienation is of relevance to political science in so far as its effects may be a lack of political integration, a failure of political socialisation, apathy toward political events and a loss of support for the political system.

☛ ANOMIE; POLITICAL PSYCHOLOGY; POLITICAL SOCIALISATION

Allegiance

In its political usage, it refers to the duties and attachments expected of every member of a political community, be it the state, or some lower order political entity such as a municipality, a party or an interest group.

In origin, it derives from the feudal practice of requiring symbolic acts of homage to one's superior. Today allegiance is presumed of all citizens, but may be overtly symbolised in some cases, e.g. the oath of allegiance by an alien on acquiring citizenship through naturalisation, or the symbolic acts of allegiance in the ceremonies of the Coronation and the Investiture of the Prince of Wales.

☛ ALIEN

Alliance

The union of two or more persons or groups for the joint pursuit of some agreed goal. In political science it is generally used in relation to the union of party (or other group) leaders for the achievement of some policy or the winning of power; to the linking of two or more parties to form a government or to pass or oppose some legislative proposal; and to offensive and defensive pacts or treaties, entered into by states, agreeing to the commitment of armed forces should any one member state be attacked, or should member states agree on a pre-emptive war.

The term 'alliance', at least in party politics, is generally reserved for application restrictively to unions for limited purposes, whereas the word 'coalition' is applied to unions for a wider range of goals, e.g. the formation of a government or the general processes of policy-making and administration.

☛ BLOC; COALITION; PACT; TREATY

Allocation

☞ POLITICAL SYSTEM; SYSTEMS ANALYSIS

Alternative vote system

A system of election in which, where there are more than two candidates competing for one office, the voter numbers his preferences among the several candidates as 1, 2, 3, . . . etc. A majority (50 per cent plus one vote) is required for election. If no candidate secures a majority of first preferences, the candidate with the least first preferences is eliminated from the poll, and his second preferences are used as a means of distributing his votes among the remaining candidates. Should this redistribution still not suffice to produce a majority for one candidate, the next lowest candidate in terms of first preferences is eliminated, with his second preferences being redistributed (plus the *third* preferences of any redistributed second preferences he has gained already), and the process continues until one candidate has the necessary majority.

Example: with five candidates competing for office, and 200 votes cast (majority = 101 votes), the first preferences were:

ABLE	85
BROWN	65
CASS	25
DOODY	15
EVANS	10

Evans's second preferences are given as 5 to ABLE and 5 to DOODY, thus the voting after redistribution stands as:

ABLE	$85 + 5 = 90$
BROWN	$65 + 0 = 65$
CASS	$25 + 0 = 25$
DOODY	$15 + 5 = 20$

Doody's 15 second preferences are given as follows: 10 to ABLE and 5 to BROWN, and his 5 votes from Evans's second preferences all give ABLE as their third preference. Thus:

ABLE	$85 + 5 + (10 + 5) = 105$ (elected)
BROWN	$65 + 0 + (5 + 0) = 70$
CASS	$25 + 0 + (0 + 0) = 25$

Variations of this system can exist which weight first preferences in some way, or which use second and subsequent ballots on separate occasions, following the elimination of the bottom candidates.

☛ ELECTORAL SYSTEM; PROPORTIONAL REPRESENTATION; SECOND BALLOT SYSTEM

Analogies

Similarities or resemblances which are identified concerning relevant qualities of two or more otherwise dissimilar things. Analogies are used in social science as heuristic devices (e.g. the analogies between political power and money, or between the 'political market' in which votes are exchanged for promised outputs of political policies and activities, and the 'economic market' in which money is exchanged for goods and services). They may form the basis of models. The cybernetic model of political communication used by Karl Deutsch (see *The Nerves of Government*, New York, Free Press, 1963) is an analogical model.

Care must be taken over the selection of analogies to ensure that the requisite similarities are in fact similar with respect to the problem under investigation, otherwise false analogies will occur, leading to spurious results.

☛ MODEL

Anarchy

The organisation of society on the basis of voluntary cooperation, and especially without the agency of political institutions, i.e. the state. It relies on what its proponents believe is the essential goodness of man's nature and his willingness to cooperate with his fellows for mutual benefit, and it rejects the artificiality and the corrupting influence of political organisation, especially in its coercive aspects.

☛ SOCIETY; STATE

Annexation

The act of adding some new territory to that already held by a state, by treaty, force, or other means, for the purposes of establishing political rule over that area. Examples: Texas was annexed by the United States in 1845, Sudetenland was annexed by Germany in 1938, and Israel passed legislation annexing the Jordanian areas of Jerusalem in August 1967, following the Six Day War.

☛ CESSION

Anomie

A term, first used by Durkheim (e.g. in his classic study *Suicide*), which indicates a social situation in which the individual is disoriented towards society because of an apparent absence of, or a conflict among, norms to guide his social behaviour, giving rise to unhappiness, deviant behaviour, even perhaps to suicide. Other scholars, such as Merton and Parsons, have extended the notion to include situations where there is conflict for the individual between social goals and socially acceptable means of attaining those goals.

For political situations, anomie is important as being a possible factor in political behaviour (leading to deviant political behaviour, extremist groups, etc.), and as being more likely to occur in times of political change such as periods of revolution, rapid political development, civil war, etc.

☛ ALIENATION; NORM

Anti-Semitism

Antagonism toward the Jewish race, religion and culture, in form ranging from an incoherent prejudice, often undeclared, to a quite explicit ideology.

Examples may be found from pre-Christian times, but in its more explicit and modern forms it dates from late-nineteenth-century Russian practices. The rise to power of the Nazi Party in Germany led to anti-Semitism becoming official government policy, typified by the Nuremberg Laws. Manifestations of anti-Semitism have been found in most countries where Jews have settled, and its central complaints have been religious rivalry, economic competition, and the desire for ethnic and cultural homogeneity. It is distinct from anti-Zionism, but was a major contributory factor to the rise of Zionism.

☛ ZIONISM

Apathy

A lack of concern, or indifference towards something. In politics, it refers to some state of uninterestedness towards political issues or choices, revealed most clearly by a failure to vote, or to express an opinion when given an opportunity to do so, e.g. in an opinion survey.

It should be noted that failure to vote or express an opinion does not always necessarily involve apathy; such failure may arise from different reasons, some of which may include high levels of political interest.

☞ ABSTENTION

Apportionment

The process of dividing a territory into areas (constituencies) for the purpose of holding elections or selecting delegates, and at the same time allocating to each area the number of seats in the elected body to which it is entitled.

Apportionment often takes account of the distribution of population among existing communities, the existence of natural boundaries, and the densities of population, but the laws or regulations under which it takes place generally require each area to possess equal (or near-equal) populations or electorates, except where specific differential requirements are stated (e.g. the distribution of seats in the West German *Bundesrat*, or the minimum of one Representative per state, irrespective of population, in the US Congress).

The word is also applied to non-territorial allocations of seats on bodies such as professional associations, political party structures, or trade unions.

☞ CONSTITUENCY; GERRYMANDERING;
REAPPORTIONMENT

Area studies

A term similar to, and sometimes used interchangeably with, 'regional studies', involving the intensive study of the languages, cultures and societies of a specified region or area, such as the Middle East, South-east Asia or Eastern Europe. Such studies often involve several disciplines, and in some universities are supported through special centres for the study of particular areas.

☞ REGIONAL STUDIES (B): international regions

Aristocracy

Rule by 'the best', i.e. by an elite selected (perhaps self-selected) according to their supposed possession of some monopoly of certain qualities or superiority of attributes deemed to be desirable in a group of rulers. Such superiority is often based on, or supported by, cultural traditions.

These qualities or attributes vary, but in the past aristocracies have been suggested, or have existed, based on wisdom (Plato's *Republic*), race (in South Africa, Rhodesia, Nazi Germany's occupied territories), birth within a privileged class, often based on landed property (feudal and postfeudal Britain), and caste (political communities in India at various periods).

☛ CASTE; ELITE; OLIGARCHY; TECHNOCRACY

Articulation of interests

☞ INTEREST ARTICULATION

Attitude scaling

A method for the measurement, and hence the comparison, of intensity or strength of attitudes, as expressed by verbal statements.

The method associated with Thurstone was to obtain the opinion of 'judges' as to a large number of statements held to be connected with the attitude under study, in relation to a scale ranging from 'extremely favourable' to 'extremely unfavourable'. An assortment of these statements was then selected for use in testing attitudes, chosen so that the full range of positions on the scale was represented. Respondents were then given a score on the basis of their agreement or disagreement with the statements. The Lickert scale modified this method by allowing respondents to indicate the strength of their agreement or disagreement with selected statements. The Guttman 'scaling' technique is based on a preliminary ordering of statements considered to be relevant to the attitude in question, such that agreement with a later statement will tend to be associated with agreement on all earlier questions. Paired statements may also be used for the construction of attitude scales. Here the respondent selects one of two statements in each of a number of cases as being the more representative of his attitude towards a particular object or phenomenon. The 'semantic differential', developed by Osgood and his collaborators, is a series of scales (usually consisting of seven points) on which the subject is asked to place the concept corresponding to the attitude under investigation; the scales are labelled with pairs of opposites, usually adjectives such as 'good:bad', 'strong:weak', etc.

Scaling presupposes that an attitude can be measured, at least ordinally, on a single dimension.

Attitude scaling has found a number of applications in political analysis, including opinion surveys of electors in advance of an electoral campaign, attitudes of legislators to a series of related bills, attitudes of judges to cases involving e.g. reinterpretation of constitutional law, etc.

☛ ATTITUDES

Attitudes

Sets of relatively persistent orientations which an individual possesses with regard to situations or objects, which are expressive of the person's preferences or valuation of those situations or objects, and which tend to be internally consistent. Being mental states, they are inferred from the behaviour (including the verbal behaviour) of the person regarding the situation or object concerned, e.g. the United Nations; the war in Vietnam; desegregation policies.

Attitudes are distinguishable from ideologies, in that ideologies are less specific, and may involve—and influence the content of —many attitudes; they differ from motivations, in so far as attitudes are relatively permanent, though they may be themselves the motivation of conduct in a particular situation, and also motivations may not be associated with attitudes in every case, e.g. they may be relative to specific events (stimuli), or efforts to reduce tension arising from 'drives'. An opinion is an expression of some part of the content of an attitude.

Attitude measurement, or attitude scaling, is carried on by means of the observation, classification and analysis of behaviour held to be expressive of a particular attitude or attitudes. Such measurement is concerned with e.g. the intensity, content and consistency of attitudes. Besides these, other important areas of research into attitudes are those concerned with the formation and the alteration of attitudes over time.

In politics, attitudes are important in many fields, e.g. voting behaviour; decision-making; support for regimes and their policies; political integration; etc.

☛ ATTITUDE SCALING; IDEOLOGY; MOTIVATION; OPINION; STEREOTYPE; VALUES

13 A

Audience

The people who are, or are intended to be, the receivers of specified messages. In political science the term is used particularly in studies of political communication, and various devices for the identification and measurement of audiences for particular messages, or messages put out by particular media, have been developed. However, the degrees of attention given by members of an audience, or the relationships between message content and audience behaviour—both of which involve psychological as well as political analysis—are more complex and, so far, less developed areas of research.

☛ POLITICAL COMMUNICATION

Autarchy

Used in a political context, autarchy means the ability to govern one's own state, and is thus a synonym for autonomy. In economic usage it refers to a state of economic self-sufficiency.

☛ AUTONOMY

Authority

Authority, while associated with concepts such as power, influence and leadership, has its own distinctive meaning. Like these related concepts, authority is a basis for the securing of assent or compliance concerning a decision or course of action. The distinction rests on the nature of the grounds of such assent or compliance. With power, it is ultimately the contingent operation of coercive sanctions; with influence, it is some directly persuasive reason or attitude; with leadership, it is reliance on some form of accepted superiority. However, the basis of authority seems to be the ability to secure assent or compliance on the grounds of legitimate superiority in relation to not simply performance (which may be the basis of e.g. charismatic leadership) but the basic values of society also. Such basic values, embodied by abridgement in an 'authoritative' person, institution, decision or action, thus provide the linkage between legitimacy and authority, and to the otherwise unhelpful definition of authority as the exercise of 'legitimate' power.

Political science is concerned generally with the sources, conditions and exercise of power and authority, but it also has certain specific areas of interest in relation to the empirical study of authority. Among these are:

the operation of authority relationships in specific political contexts;

the classification of types or styles of authority;

the psychological roots of the acceptance and the exercise of authority;

the distribution of authority institutions in the political system, and their coordination and conflict.

☛ LEADERSHIP; LEGITIMACY; POWER

Autocracy

A system of government in which one man, or a group of men with a clearly identifiable leader, exercises political power without effective legal or customary constraints, and without responsibility to an electorate or any other political body. Such power may be considered to be exercised legitimately only if there is reason to suppose that it is not maintained wholly by coercion. Examples of autocrats: Stalin; Hitler; President Duvalier of Haiti.

☛ ABSOLUTISM; AUTHORITY; DICTATORSHIP

Autonomy

The ability to be self-governing, often in a context which suggests pressures to change or prevent this.

☛ AUTARCHY

Axiom

A proposition in scientific analysis which is to be regarded as self-evident, requiring no further proof; a basic statement which forms part of the fundamentals of a scientific discipline, and from which hypotheses, laws and theories may be developed.

B

Ballot

The process by which votes are gathered from those qualified to vote; also, the vote itself. The secret ballot is any process by which votes are cast in such a way that the identity of the voter is not able to be connected (at least without exceedingly complex legal formalities, as in Britain) with the vote he has cast.

☛ ELECTION; ELECTORAL SYSTEM; VOTING

Bandwagon effect

The idea that the publication of predictions of the outcome of an election, especially in the form of opinion poll results, can cause an increase in support for the candidate or party stated to be ahead, and that this increase would not otherwise have occurred, or would have been smaller in extent, if the prediction had not been published.

An attempt to investigate this effect mathematically was made by H. Simon in his article 'Bandwagon and underdog effects of political prediction', *Public Opinion Quarterly*, xviii, 1954.

☛ UNDERDOG EFFECT

Bargaining theory

The study of negotiation (including political negotiation) by means of various approaches, formal models, theories, etc. Among these are game theory, small group experimentation, formal analysis derived from economics, conflict studies and psychological approaches.

Among the topics of major interest in the study of political bargaining are the institutional context in which bargaining occurs; the values of the parties involved; the methods of communication of bargaining moves; the possibilities of salient solutions being accepted; the methods of completion of the bargaining process; etc.

Two studies which cover many of these areas are T. Schelling, *The Strategy of Conflict*, Harvard University Press, 1960, and A. Kuhn, *The Study of Society*, Tavistock Publications, 1966, part v: 'Transactions'.

☛ CONFLICT APPROACH; ECONOMIC APPROACHES TO POLITICS; GAME THEORY

Behavioural approach

An approach to the analysis and explanation of political phenomena, which is sometimes also referred to as 'behaviouralism', and which is particularly associated with the work of American political scientists in the period after the Second World War, though its roots may be traced back to the work of Wallas and Bentley before the First World War.

This approach concentrates on the study of political behaviour itself, but not exclusively so, and the term 'behavioural' has been applied by some writers, often in a critical sense, to such diverse approaches as those of Talcott Parsons, David Truman and Karl Deutsch. Such a catholic usage of the term emphasises its major features, which may be summarised as: the attempt to generate and test verifiable scientific explanations about politics, its structures, processes, and behaviour within those structures; an emphasis on quantification and operational definitions; the avoidance of prescriptive statement and an attempt to eliminate the influences of the personal values of the investigator on his research; an open attitude to concepts, theories and approaches from other disciplines, especially those of other behavioural sciences, and a willingness to engage in interdisciplinary research; a feedback between empirical research and methodological improvement;

a comparative, and, where appropriate, cross-cultural range of inquiry.

This approach is thus a rejection of the formalism and normative orientations of the philosophic-legalistic schools which had dominated the discipline before the Second World War. It also rejects any definition of political science that confines it exclusively to the study of the state.

While not rejecting the possibility of the construction of comprehensive theories of political explanation, the practitioners of the behavioural approach take the view that such theories must wait on the establishment of trustworthy explanations of a lower level of generality. It is thus low-level or medium-level empiricism that is the main distinguishing mark of the behavioural approach, and which makes it less than congruent with the wider term: political science.

The historical development of the behavioural approach is outlined in the article by R. Dahl, 'The behavioural approach in political science: epitaph for a monument to a successful protest', *American Political Science Review*, lv, 1961.

☛ POLITICAL ANALYSIS; POLITICAL BEHAVIOUR; POLITICAL SCIENCE

Behaviouralism

☞ BEHAVIOURAL APPROACH

Bicameral

Possessing two chambers; thus normally used to describe legislatures that are organised on a two-chamber basis. Examples include: the United Kingdom Parliament; the United States Congress; most of the state legislatures in the USA; the French National Assembly; the West German *Bundestag* and *Bundesrat;* the Supreme Soviet of the USSR.

A bicameral legislature is found in most federal states. While often divided into an 'upper' and a 'lower' house, bicameral legislatures do not necessarily consist of a 'superior' chamber and an 'inferior' chamber in terms of legislative or other political powers.

☛ UNICAMERAL

Bipolarity

A situation in which the elements tend to cluster around two extreme positions on some scale. In politics it is used in two major contexts: international relations and electoral behaviour. In international relations bipolarity describes the tendency for states to group into two opposed blocs or sets of alliances, and in particular is applied to the post-1945 'cold war' situation, in which the USA and USSR were seen as leaders of two opposed groups of states and all other states were regarded either as members of one or other camp, or as uncommitted neutrals. Whether this was a useful concept even in the 1950s may be doubted; since the rise of China to the status of a major power, and the resurgence of a more independent western European policy position (based to a considerable extent on the European Economic Community), it is no longer in the least descriptive of the state of international relations. In electoral terminology bipolarity is the situation in which voters tend to choose between two major and opposed political parties, to the exclusion of minor or central parties. This is sometimes less precisely referred to as polarisation.

☛ MULTIPOLARITY; POLARISATION

Black box technique

Any analytical technique that employs the concept of a 'black box' to refer to some complex set of interactions. This 'black box' is then characterised in the analysis only by its inputs and outputs, ignoring, for the purposes of the analysis, the detailed conversion processes that go on within the 'black box'.

The technique has been used in e.g. psychological and behavioural analysis, organisational analysis, systems approaches in political analysis, etc. An example in the analysis of a political system would be to designate the legislature as a 'black box' into which demands flow as inputs and decisions emerge as outputs, ignoring the procedures by which the transformation occurs. This may be on the grounds that, for instance, such processes of transformation are overcomplex or irrelevant for the purposes of that particular analysis.

Bloc

An alliance of political actors, such as legislators, delegates, committee members, who tend to vote on a range of matters in a similar way, and who may also meet to discuss such matters, coordinate tactics for debate, etc. A bloc is independent of, and may cut across, more formal groupings such as parties. Thus, in the United States Senate there is a 'Southern bloc', and in the United Nations Organisation General Assembly several blocs exist such as the Arab bloc and the Communist bloc.

The term is also applied to alliances or groupings in international politics, e.g. the western bloc of European and American states, based on the North Atlantic Treaty Organisation.

☛ ALLIANCE; COALITION; FACTION; POLITICAL PARTY

Block voting

A system of voting in which delegates vote on behalf of the group they represent, by means of multiple votes weighted according to the size of the membership the delegate represents. It is used in Britain, for instance, at party and trade union conferences.

☛ VOTING

Bolshevism

The name given to the particular ideological and practical interpretation of Marxist ideas which was undertaken by the victorious branch of the Russian Social Democratic Labour Party, following the split from the Mensheviks in 1903. The word 'Bolshevik' refers to the *majority* which supported Lenin's ideological position at the Second Congress of the Party held in Brussels and London; 'Menshevik' refers to the *minority* group at that Congress.

In Russia the term Bolshevism is now used almost interchangeably with the terms socialism, Marxism and Leninism. The second revolution of 1917 is often called the Bolshevik revolution, since it is from that occasion that the ideas of the Bolshevists have been implemented as the official ideology of Russian governments.

☛ COMMUNISM; MARXISM; SOCIALISM

'Bossism'

A term, originating from American state and city politics but now applied in other political systems as well, used to designate the forms of leadership and organisation in which a politician uses patronage, a strong political personality, an organisational machine based on personal loyalty, strong—often violent—sanctions, and sometimes corrupt inducements for the purposes of obtaining and retaining political power. This power need not necessarily be used to obtain office for the 'boss' himself, though most bosses hold some office which provides them with a formal power base. Though generally associated with a particular political party, 'bossism' is basically uninterested in the furtherance of policy goals, except in so far as they strengthen or weaken the power of the leader.

The success of such leadership is threatened by the growth in the influence and importance of the mass media in politics, especially for a literate population; the increasing saliency of policy issues for the electorate; the centralisation of party organisation; and the improved legal regulation of electoral campaigns and procedures.

Examples of leaders who have been referred to as 'bosses': in the USA, Mark Hanna of Ohio; Frank Hague of Jersey City; and the various 'chieftains' of Tammany Hall, the New York Democratic Party headquarters; in Britain, Alderman Salvidge, leader of the Liverpool Conservatives in the period following the First World War; while in African and Asian politics many cases have been identified of powerful local leaders who have acted as 'bosses' of local party machines.

☛ LEADERSHIP; 'MACHINE POLITICS'

Boundary

A concept used in the systems approaches to political analysis, which indicates the limits of a system and the points or interfaces at which influences from other systems (the 'environment') impinge upon that system.

Boundary exchange is the process whereby inputs from other systems (e.g. demands) are matched by outputs from the political system (e.g. policies) across the boundaries of the political system.

☛ ENVIRONMENT; INPUT-OUTPUT ANALYSIS;
  POLITICAL SYSTEM; SYSTEMS ANALYSIS

Boundary exchange

☞ BOUNDARY

Budget

At the level of the state, or local government authority, the budget is the statement of expected revenues in the light of the proposed taxes, levies and other income, and proposed expenditures, usually for a twelve-month period. But it is more than a mere balance-sheet; the importance of budgetary policies, signified by the status of the finance minister of most countries and the jealousy with which legislatures guard their privileges of initiating and debating the budget, lies in its interconnection with the political programme of the government. Since most policies cost money, or are concerned with its redistribution, control of the budget is, in a very real sense, control of the executive branch of government.

New forms of budgetary presentation (e.g. long-term budgeting; planning-programming-budgeting systems—PPBS) have been developed to improve the possibility of such control. The development of specialised committees of the legislature (called variously the estimates committee, the appropriations committee, etc.) is also intended to improve control of the government through control of the budget.

☛ PLANNING-PROGRAMMING-BUDGETING SYSTEMS (PPBS)

Bureaucracy

In general usage, the term refers to any set of governmental (or other administrative) officials, possessed of certain traits of excessive formality, the use of verbiage and jargon as the basis of communication, inflexibility of procedure, and insistence on the powers—and limitations—of their office, in other words, 'red tape'.

In social science, the concept is both more specific and neutral, being used to refer to a particular pattern of administrative behaviour, associated with certain types of social organisation, and identifiable by reference to a constellation of objective criteria. Usually associated with political administration, it can also denote a form of religious, industrial, educational or other categories of administrative organisation.

The classic statement of bureaucracy as a social phenomenon is that of Max Weber (see his *Economy and Society*, ed. G. Roth and C. Wittich, vol. iii, New York, Bedminster Press, 1968, ch. 11 'Bureaucracy'). He identifies the following criteria of bureaucratic organisation: official jurisdictional areas, laid down by laws or rules; the principle of office hierarchy, involving clear lines of supervision of lower offices by higher offices; work based upon the preservation of written records ('files'); training and specialisation of personnel in office management skills; the devotion of the full attention of officials to their official activity, at least during the stated hours of their employment; the existence of procedural rules, defined, generalised, and able to be learned by all officials.

Bureaucracy, according to Weber's analytic scheme, thus involves a career-based, appointed administrative service, of fixed status and tenure, with salary linked to rank and a known rank-order of advancement. It also presupposes certain features of society, such as the development of a monetary economy, large-scale organisation of tasks and resources, the availability of modern methods of communication, cultural acceptance of 'rationality' in administrative decision-making and of legal authority as the basis of legitimation of leadership, and a tendency to centralisation of power. In turn, bureaucracy has its own effects on social organisation; among these are a tendency toward its own perpetuation, consequential educational changes directed toward recruitment to the bureaucratic domain based on expertise, and a tendency toward the democratisation of political life, probably on a 'mass party' basis, as a result of the establishment of rationality in decision-making and open recruitment to administrative positions.

A useful survey of aspects of bureaucracy is that of R. Merton *et al.*, eds., *Reader in Bureaucracy*, New York, Free Press, 1952.

☛ ADMINISTRATION; PUBLIC ADMINISTRATION

C

Cabinet

The committee of leading ministers of the government, for the purposes of confidentially discussing the business of the executive, taking the political decisions necessary to deal with pending business and formulating new policies. Generally it is presided over by the head of state or the prime minister (or equivalent officer). It is found in most western democracies, and in many developing countries also.

Membership is generally confined to the ministers of major departments, but certain other leading politicians may be included on the basis of their personal standing in the government.

The power—and thus the collective political responsibility—of the cabinet varies from country to country. It is very powerful in Britain, less so in France and West Germany, even less so in the USA. In one-party states it is either absent as an institution, or it possesses little power due to the political competition afforded by the central committee of the party.

In France, the *cabinet* of a minister refers to the small group of personal staff appointed by a minister to advise and assist him in his department.

☞ CABINET GOVERNMENT

Cabinet government

A system of government which is marked by the existence of a cabinet which collectively decides on the policies to be presented to the legislature, assumes collective responsibility for those policies before the legislature, and is also responsible for the implementation of policy through the control and coordination of the executive departments. In such a system, the cabinet must therefore possess the support of a majority in the legislature which is sufficiently stable for the bulk of its policies to receive legislative assent. It also presupposes a separation of the offices of head of state and leader of the government.

It is often contrasted with presidential government, in which the head of state is also the head of the government, and in which the cabinet is used as an advisory rather than a responsible body. The United Kingdom and Australia are examples of cabinet government; the USA is an example of presidential government.

☛ CABINET; RESPONSIBILITY

Campaign

A process of persuasion aimed at a body of decision-makers, intended to bring about the appointment or election of a person to some political office, or to secure the adoption or rejection of some principle or policy. In either case regulations may exist restricting the methods, timing or costs of campaigning.

Candidate

One who is put forward for election or appointment to an office, and who is not disqualified by reason of failure to meet some necessary condition of either personal status (e.g. age, sex, membership of a proscribed institution), or process (e.g. the presentation of proper nomination papers, the submission of any required financial deposit). In other words, a mere aspirant is not properly a candidate if there are legal barriers to his election or appointment.

Capitalism

The economic system in which the greater part of the economy is controlled by private (i.e. non-state) owners, relying on the private provision of capital investment in return for distributed profits. Its proponents believe that such a system tends to maximise the satisfaction of economic needs by providing for the most rational distribution of economic resources.

The operation of such a system has certain implications for the political organisation of the state, though there is no necessary equation between capitalism and democracy. In effect, capitalism envisages the functions of the state as being limited to the mainten-ance of external security and internal law and order. Some authorities would go further and claim that the state under a capitalist system also has the responsibility of removing any structural hindrances to the operation of private enterprise, e.g. by legislating against monopolies and restrictive practices. The provision of welfare services by the state, or its claims to regulate the economy by measures of planning, nationalisation, or budget-ary policies are thus regarded as various degrees of interference with the operation of a pure capitalist system.

'State capitalism' is the term sometimes used to refer to economic systems in which large-scale production operates in major sectors, regulated and protected to a large extent by the state, but in which a major aim of production remains the creation and distribution (including distribution to the state) of a financial surplus.

☛ MARXISM; POLITICAL ECONOMY; SOCIALISM;
SYNDICALISM; WELFARE STATE

Case study method

A systematic method of analysis which depends on the deliberate and detailed study of 'cases' (i.e. in political science, of such specific phenomena as groups, e.g. political parties; processes, e.g. the making of a policy or the course of a revolution; and individual behaviour, e.g. the decisions of a political leader).

The chief purposes of the case study method are: as a teaching device, to enable students to examine the fullest possible range of variables and data involved in an example of a particular type of political phenomenon; as a research method, to derive and to test hypotheses and relationships by the thorough examination of detailed cases.

Cases may be studied by any combination of a wide variety of methods and approaches, e.g. interviews, documentary ana-lysis, simulation, game theory, gaming and comparative analysis.

Examples of the use of the case study method in political

science: H. Eckstein, *Pressure Group Politics: the case of the British Medical Association*, Allen & Unwin, 1960; K. Lamb and P. Smith, *Campaign Decision-Making: The Presidential Election of 1964*, Belmont, USA, Wadsworth, 1968; R. Dahl, *Who Governs? Democracy and power in an American city*, Yale University Press, 1961.

Caste

A category denoting the social status of its members, in which status is permanent and determined from birth, and often based on religious prescription. Members of the same caste are expected to intermarry, thus perpetuating the caste system, and in some caste systems certain social functions are associated with each caste. Contact with members of other castes is usually severely restricted.

While it is difficult to find any pure examples of an operative caste system among large-scale societies today, the Hindu population of India was, and to some extent remains, stratified according to caste. In such cases, caste may be an important influence on, e.g., voting habits and other forms of political participation.

☞ ARISTOCRACY; SOCIAL CLASS; SOCIAL STRUCTURE; STATUS

Caucus

A private gathering of leaders and other influential members of a political party, faction or other such group, for the purposes of selecting candidates for electoral campaigns (especially at the local level; the nominating caucus was a predecessor of the nominating convention in American politics, for example); discussion of matters pending before a legislative or other policy-making body; the settlement of political strategies, etc.

Usually the term denotes such an inner party group where its power within the party is strong, and its decisions become binding on members of the party organisation at the level at which it acts (e.g. in the national legislature; city council level; local politics; etc), and even, in some cases, may be binding on members in office (e.g. in a cabinet or in a coalition government). Though associated particularly with American and Australian politics, the term has been applied in British and other contexts. It is especially appropriate as applied to some party organisations at the local level in British politics.

☞ FACTION; POLITICAL PARTY

Cell

A small organised group of a political party or movement, usually of a clandestine nature, and often based on a neighbourhood or work place. The term is applied particularly to units of organisation in the Communist Party in various countries, though officially abandoned in the USSR in 1939.

Centralisation

The process of concentrating political powers more closely in some single central decision-making body, e.g. by transferring responsibilities from federal units to the federal government, or the withdrawal of delegated powers from subordinate agencies.

☛ DECENTRALISATION; DEVOLUTION

Cession

The act of voluntarily rendering up territory over which the ruler, or the government, had authority, to some other ruler or state. This may be e.g. part of a peace settlement, an exchange of territory, an item in a royal marriage contract, a sale for monetary consideration, etc. Though circumstances may impel a ruler to cede territory, the act itself must be, in form at least, one of voluntary choice to differentiate it from conquest.

Examples of cession: the return of Alsace-Lorraine to France by Germany under the Versailles Treaty, 1919; the purchase by the USA of the Virgin Islands from Denmark, 1917; the 'Louisiana Purchase' of 1803.

☛ ANNEXATION; TREATY

Charisma

The extraordinary qualities of an innovative or revolutionary leader, based on belief by his followers in his possession of e.g. religious or magical powers. The term can be applied, by extension, to symbols or institutions connected with such leadership. It is derived from the Greek term meaning 'gift of grace.'

The continuance of charisma depends on the successful accomplishment of extraordinary achievements; failure to achieve publicised goals may diminish the belief of followers, and of the leader himself, in his charismatic powers, and his overthrow becomes likely.

The term is used in Weber's typology of leadership. The other two 'ideal types' are traditional leadership, based on habit, and rational-legal leadership, based on interest. Since all these are ideal types of leadership, most examples of leaders will be a mixture of these types.

Hitler, Nkrumah, Nasser, Mao Tse-tung and Fidel Castro are usually among those cited as examples of charismatic leaders.

☛ AUTHORITY; LEADERSHIP; LEGITIMACY

Chi-square test

A statistical test used to indicate the probabilities that differences between actual measurements and expected measurements are due to chance, or are statistically significant. It is employed, for instance, in the analysis of sample survey data to indicate the reliability of the results obtained.

☛ SAMPLE; STATISTICAL ANALYSIS; SURVEY

Christian democracy

An ideological movement which provides the basic orientation for conservative parties in several European and Latin American states where the Catholic faith is strong. Examples include the MRP (*Mouvement Républicain Populaire*) in France, the People's Party in Austria, the Christian Democrats in Italy and West Germany, the Social Christian Party in Venezuela.

Historically, the movement stems from the Catholic parties of the nineteenth century, though since the second world war it has lost its exclusive association with Catholicism in some countries. Its principles tend toward a conservative attitude on economic affairs, especially concerning property rights, a hostility toward socialism and Communism, a moderately liberal stance on social reform, and a more or less formal commitment to Christian doctrine and ethics.

There is in existence a Christian Democratic international organisation, which holds periodic conferences and acts as a co-ordinating body.

☛ CONFESSIONAL PARTIES; PARTY

Citizen

A member of a state who is entitled to such civil and political rights as exist in that state, and owes obligations in respect of those rights, as contrasted to other residents who do not possess such rights or obligations. The extent to which citizenship is conferred in a state depends on its form of government. In some states in the past, only the wealthy or those of high birth have been regarded as citizens; in others, women have been excluded; in yet others, religion or ethnic grouping have been made tests. Slaves were not regarded as citizens in e.g. ancient Greece or pre-civil-war America.

In most states there exists a body of law relating to citizenship, which is used to decide disputed cases and which includes in its codes definitions of citizenship and the status of non-citizens.

☛ ALIEN; CIVIL RIGHTS

City

Commonly, any densely populated large urban concentration. More strictly, certain states (e.g. states of the United States of America, Canada) apply various standards of population size, area, etc., to any town wishing to be granted the title and form of 'city'. In Britain there was a customary early correspondence between cities and the sites of cathedrals, but this equivalence no longer entirely holds. Though British cities receive royal charters, these are only of a dignifying nature, and confer no legal or administrative privileges. There is no necessary connection between cities and county or municipal boroughs, for instance.

☛ CONURBATION; METROPOLIS

Civil disobedience

A deliberate refusal on the part of a citizen, or a group of citizens, to comply with a legitimate order or regulation of the government, in order to draw attention to some grievance or to secure some political end. The grievance may be that the order itself is immoral or unethical, or simply impolitic; indeed, it is often the case with acts of civil disobedience that the legitimacy of the order itself is questioned.

Examples of civil disobedience include the campaigns of Mahatma Gandhi against British rule in India (e.g. over the salt laws in

1930); the activities of some sections of the Campaign for Nuclear Disarmament in Britain; and the civil rights 'sit-ins' in the southern states of the USA, 1960–62.

☛ DIRECT ACTION; LEGITIMACY; REBELLION

Civil-military relations

The study of the political and social influences on, and effects of, the armed forces in society is often termed the study of civil-military relations. It includes the study of the political control of the armed forces (which, in a militarised state, may be by the military itself); the role of military officers as an elite in the polity; the armed forces as an interest with potential influence on the policy process; the active intervention of the armed forces in the making and changing of governments and regimes; the military as a developmental agent; and the effects of war on the political order of society.

While also of interest to the legal and sociological sciences, problems of civil-military relations are fundamentally political problems, at least in so far as there are elements of public policy involved.

☛ COUP D'ÉTAT; DICTATORSHIP; ELITE; FASCISM;
MILITARISM; PUTSCH; WAR

Civil rights

Those freedoms and privileges within a society which belong to the citizen, and thus the denial of which is regarded as a denial of the status of citizen. The details of which rights and privileges fall into this category vary from society to society, and from time to time.

If civil rights are in some manner called into question, it is the duty of the courts to resolve any disputes. If it is felt that existing civil rights are insufficient or inappropriate, it is the task of the legislature to amend them by statute. If the protection offered by statute, constitution, customary practice or other source of civil rights is inoperative, this is a failure of the administrative branch, and recourse to the courts may be necessary.

A United Nations Declaration of Human Rights enumerates a basic list of civil rights, which it believes should be available in all states. In Britain, such rights have been primarily a matter of custom and tradition, though some statutory statements exist (e.g. the Bill of Rights, 1689). In France the preamble to the Constitution of the Fifth Republic refers to the Declaration of the Rights of Man of 1789 as the French source of civil rights. In the USA such rights are based on various articles of, and amendments to, the Constitution, and legislation interpreting, amplifying and implementing those rights (e.g. the Civil Rights Acts of 1960 and 1964).

☞ CITIZEN

Civil war

The occurrence of armed hostilities between two (or more) relatively large sections of a society, both possessed of political organisation, and both claiming the right to rule the society, or alternatively in the case of one of the parties, the right to independent status. A civil war is therefore distinguished from a rebellion by these claims to political power on the part of the insurrectionary party, and distinguished from a revolution by the approximate balance of forces on each side, though a revolution may precede, accompany or follow a civil war. Examples of civil wars include those in the USA (1861–65), Russia after 1917, Spain (1936–39) and Nigeria following the secession of Biafra.

☞ INSURRECTION; REBELLION; REVOLUTION; WAR

Classification

The process of grouping items or phenomena on the basis of some stipulated quality which they share. Such classification can be based on the presence or absence of a factor (e.g. monarchies and non-monarchies; male and female members of a legislature), or categories of degree (e.g. one-party, two-party and multi-party systems, or the categorisation of electoral constituencies as safe, competitive and marginal on the basis of the percentage 'swing' needed to capture the seat from the incumbent party).

The utility of a classification depends basically on the precision of the categories used in relation to the purpose of classification; in addition, an efficient classificatory scheme requires that no item should belong in more than one category, and that no item under consideration should be omitted from the scheme of classification.

Classifications are used to generate hypotheses, to order information, to suggest areas of investigation, etc., and they are themselves modified by the testing of hypotheses.

☛ ORDERING; TYPOLOGY

Cleavage

The condition of division between members of a political group or political system, and thus the opposite of 'consensus'. Cleavage may be caused by disagreement over political goals, means of attaining them, attitudes, ideology, leadership, procedures, etc. It may be inherent in the composition of the political collectivity, e.g. in a racially divided society, or between adherents of different religious faiths. The purpose of political integration is to overcome cleavage to an extent sufficient for the political system to persist and function.

☛ CONSENSUS; POLITICAL INTEGRATION

Coalition

A combination of two or more different political actors (who may be, for example, individuals or political parties) in order to achieve some goal which is mutually advantageous. More particularly, it refers to a government composed of members of two or more parties, in order to secure a working majority, to reduce partisan politics in time of crisis, or for some other reason.

The analytical study of the formation and behaviour of coalitions has been an important sub-area of political analysis in recent years. In particular, it has been associated with bargaining and game theory, and with economic approaches to political behaviour. One of the most explicit essays on the analysis of coalition behaviour in political situations is W. Riker, *The Theory of Political Coalitions*, Yale University Press, 1962. In it, he investigates such propositions as: 'In social relations similar to n-person, zero-sum games with side-payments, participants create coalitions just as large as they believe will ensure winning, and no larger' (pp. 32–3). Other studies have investigated actual examples of coalition formation in political situations, as well as in artificial 'laboratory' or classroom situations, studying the effects of e.g. information, personality, and social attributes on coalition formation.

☛ ALLIANCE; BLOC; ECONOMIC APPROACHES TO
   POLITICS; GAME THEORY; SIDE PAYMENTS

Coefficient of correlation

☞ CORRELATION

Coercion

The threat or the application of force, physical or non-physical, in order to persuade some person or group to take some decision or perform some action which otherwise they would not be likely to do.

Cohesion

Cohesion is the concept of mutual attraction of two or more persons in a relationship. It is related to the values which persons place upon the functions fulfilled by their relationships, and will vary according to changes in the needs of these persons and changes in the effectiveness of the relationship. Alterations in e.g. the structure of the relationship, its communication patterns, the style of organisation in an organised-group relationship, etc., will affect the level of cohesion.

Cohesion in political relationships is a concept very similar in meaning to that of 'political integration', being the quality of attraction of members of a political community towards that community as an organisation.

☛ POLITICAL INTEGRATION

Cohort analysis

The analysis of a social collectivity in terms of sub-groupings (cohorts) based on the chronological intervals at which such sub-groupings were able to acquire certain specified characteristics. Such analysis permits the examination of temporal variations as related to some other factor, e.g. political socialisation in relation to the year of birth (the cohort), or current party preference in relation to the year in which each cohort could cast its first vote in a general election (e.g. in Britain cohorts would be labelled 1945, 1950, 1951, 1955...etc., and in the USA 1944, 1948, 1952, 1956... etc.)

☛ CROSS-SECTIONAL ANALYSIS; LONGITUDINAL
   STUDIES

Collectivism

Collectivism is the belief—directly opposed to individualism—that society should be organised on the basis of collective control (generally through the agency of state institutions) of economic production and political decisions. It is associated with various forms of socialism, Communism, syndicalism, etc., and is often related to political ideologies and systems of rule of an authoritarian type.

☛ COMMUNISM; NATIONALISATION; SOCIALISM;
   STATISM; SYNDICALISM

Colonialism

The practice of occupying, by force or by peaceful means, territory which is relatively underdeveloped, for the purposes of establishing settlers from the parent state and using the territory mainly for economic, but secondarily perhaps for political or strategic, advantage of the colonising power.

It is distinguished from imperialism by the fact that a colony is usually either uninhabited when it is acquired, or inhabited by members of a different race, whereas some of the dominions of an empire may be inhabited by members of a similar race to the imperial power, e.g. as in the Austro-Hungarian empire, and by the emphasis in colonial settlement on the economic advantage of the colonising power.

☛ COLONY; IMPERIALISM

Colonisation

☞ COLONIALISM; COLONY; IMPERIALISM

Colony

An area originally outside the boundaries of the parent state, and settled—peacefully or by force—by inhabitants of that state, to which it is also politically subordinate. A colony is settled generally for purposes of economic exploitation by the colonising state, and is usually regarded as an underdeveloped area, relative to the parent state; this situation may be perpetuated by a system of commercial exchange in which the economic interests of the colony are subordinated to those of the colonising power.

☛ COLONIALISM

Committee

A group of persons, who may be elected or nominated, derived from some larger body in order to carry out certain specific functions. It is generally smaller than the parent body, except in special cases where provision exists for a 'committee of the whole', as in the British Parliament, where all members of the House of Commons may sit but where rules of committee procedure, and not those of plenary sessions, apply.

Committees generally are required to report on their deliberations and activities to the parent body. Among the advantages of using committees are: expedition of business, since committees may sit when the plenary body does not, and may work more quickly; expertise; secrecy; an ability to deal with matters in a less formal manner than can the plenary body.

Commonwealth

Though sometimes used to refer generally to any independent political community, more specifically it is the name given to the 'free association' of states which once were part of the British Empire as colonies, dominions, etc. The term 'Commonwealth' was used administratively in the postwar years (e.g. in 1947 the Dominion Office became the Commonwealth Relations Office). There is no formal legal or constitutional agreement relating to the regulation of the Commonwealth as an institution, though several manifestations exist such as the Commonwealth Prime Ministers' Conference and Commonwealth preference in the British tariff structure.

A previous use of the term was to designate the regime of Cromwell following the English civil war (1649–60), and it is also a formal part of the title of Australia, and of some American states such as Massachusetts.

Communications approach

The communications approach is based on the view of political activity as involving a substantial degree of human communication, and that such communication is central to, and in part even determines, the actual pattern such activity assumes. The study of such communication, it is therefore postulated, may be of value in describing, classifying, analysing and explaining important aspects of political life. At the same time, the proponents of the communications approach do not claim that it is helpful in analysing every aspect of politics, e.g. it is not especially valuable in explaining ideologies, violent system changes such as revolutions, the distribution of political resources or the attainment of political goals.

It is one of many approaches developed primarily after the Second World War, which attempt to import greater rigour and precision into the study of political science by the development and testing of hypotheses and the construction of models.

The approach has developed in many directions, but is generally concerned with communication within a specified political system, between two or more political systems, or between political systems and their environment. In order to do this it attempts to identify the structures which send and receive messages; the channels which are used, along with their capacities and rates of utilisation; information storage processes; feedback mechanisms; the codes and languages employed; and the contents of messages transmitted. Many of the concepts used in the approach are derived or borrowed from information theory and communications technology, and particularly from cybernetics: the study of communication and control in systems.

In political science, the approach is especially applicable to the study of bargaining, conflict resolution, decision-making (in groups and at the level of the system itself, e.g. in general elections), evaluation of policies, propaganda, the transmission of operational information, the generation of specific and diffuse support, transactions with other subsystems of the social system (e.g. the economy, the scientific community), international relations, and political development and change.

Several research devices have been employed as part of the communications approach. Among those which have been used with some success have been: quantitative and qualitative content analysis; the measurement of international information flows; survey research; game theory; simulations and gaming; and factor analysis.

Among the major works on the theoretical basis of the communications approach are: K. Deutsch, *The Nerves of Government*, New York, Free Press, 1963, 1966, and L. Pye, *Communications and Political Development*, Princeton University Press, 1963. Other major works of relevance include: W. Schramm, *Mass Media and National Development*, Stanford University Press, 1964; J. Burton, *Conflict and Communication*, Macmillan, 1969; J. Blumler and D.

McQuail, *Television in Politics: its uses and influence*, Faber, 1968.

☛ AUDIENCE; CONTENT ANALYSIS; FEEDBACK; POLITICAL COMMUNICATION

Communism

An ideology based on the communal ownership of all property, coupled with some form of non-hierarchical political structure. In consequence, the social structure would be classless, money would be abolished, and work would be directed by, and performed willingly in the interests of, the community as a whole: 'from each according to his ability, to each according to his needs'. Except in the particular context of Marxist doctrine (see below), Communism is thus one form of socialism, differing from other forms primarily in its emphasis on social and economic change as a preliminary condition of political change, rather than as a consequence of it.

Though there are examples of pre-Marxian Communist ideas (e.g. in Plato's *Republic*, in the writings of Winstanley and the 'Diggers' *c.* 1650, in some aspects of Chartism, and in the ideas of French socialist groups in the 1840s), the first source of modern Communist ideology is the *Communist Manifesto* of Marx and Engels (1848). After the Bolshevik Revolution in Russia (1917) and in keeping with the writings of Marx, Lenin emphasised that Russia was as yet only a socialist society, and that the transition to a Communist society, accompanied by the 'withering away of the state', though part of the inevitability of the historical process, would only come when the technological and social foundations for its achievement had been established. The international hostility to Communism was also a delaying factor, which gave rise to the aim of 'socialism in one country' as an example necessary before Communism could be achieved. In Russia the ideology of Communism became elaborated by, in particular, the pronouncements and publications of Lenin and Stalin.

But Communist parties and Communist regimes developed elsewhere e.g. in Cuba and in China. Here the doctrines of Moscow were not always accepted as being true interpretations of Communism, and thus Maoist and Castroite interpretations, among others, have also become important, as have the interpretations of the exiled Trotsky, and the 'liberal Communists' of e.g. Czechoslovakia. Primarily these differences arise over the means to be employed to achieve a Communist society and the policies and social organisation (e.g. in relation to agriculture, foreign trade, industry, party organisation, civil liberties) necessary to its attainment. The international organisation of Communism in the post-war period has shown anything but a unified front. Thus any attempts at definition which go beyond the basic statements outlined above would have to be qualified by indication of the sources of interpretation used. Definitions based on national experiences are further complicated by the tendency in developing states for Communism to have become intermingled with the struggle for national self-determination, e.g. in Vietnam, Algeria, and Malaya.

☞ BOLSHEVISM; COLLECTIVISM; MARXISM;
SOCIALISM

Community

As with the terms 'society' and 'state', a wide variety of definitions exists of the word 'community'. While these tend to agree on the fact that it refers to some form of social organisation, there is no agreement as to its extent or its characteristics.

Some definitions make 'society' or 'social group' synonymous with 'community', others distinguish a community from other social aggregates by its range or extent (i.e. it may be as large as a society, while to others it refers to a smaller grouping such as a village), and by its social characteristics, in that a community is recognisable by its culture which is enjoyed by the members of the community, and the high degree of shared activity of the members that goes on within the community. This more distinctive use has the advantage of allowing a society to be defined as containing many communities.

A political community is, in these terms, definable as a social group that shares a common political culture and within which a high degree of shared political activity of the community membership takes place.

☞ COMMUNITY STUDIES; POLITICAL CULTURE;
SOCIETY; SUBCOMMUNITY

Community studies

The community, in the sense of a local territorial area containing a well-defined social system in which the bulk of the individual members' social transactions occur, has provided political science with a unit of manageable size for analysis, but of sufficient complexity to be of significance and interest. Thus 'community studies' has become an autonomous area of political science, and particularly of political sociology.

Most political studies of communities (rather than of local government) have been American, and have concentrated on aspects of community power, its structures and its methods of making decisions. The works of Floyd Hunter, Robert Dahl and Nelson Polsby have been among the most influential in building up a body of research studies in these areas. A critical survey of these studies is contained in N. Polsby, *Community Power and Political Theory*, Yale University Press, 1963. Britain, continental Europe and modernising postcolonial states have also been areas in which such studies have been undertaken.

A major problem in studies of community power has been the nature of the ruling elite, if one exists at all. The controversy has been primarily between the supporters of the 'reputational' school, who delineate community power structures by virtue of the selection of members as 'powerful' by community members, and the 'decisional' school, which stresses the identification of influence exercised by persons over the outcome of actual community decisions. Among other aspects of political life which community studies have been concerned with are membership of community organisations, and especially political organisations; ethnic differences in community politics; the structure and behaviour of political parties at the community level.

☛ COMMUNITY; ELITE; LOCAL GOVERNMENT STUDIES

Comparative analysis

A method of analysis used in political science to describe, classify and explain data by making observations of the similarities and differences to be found in the various items under analysis, e.g. constitutional courts, agrarian pressure groups, political socialisation processes, revolutionary ideologies; or in the same item over a range of time periods. From such comparison it is possible that statements concerning the causes and effects of differences and similarities may be made, classificatory schemes drawn up, and new relationships discovered. To this extent comparison is fundamental to the scientific analysis of political phenomena.

However, comparative analysis is also regarded as a specific and significant sub-area of political science, with its own methods and problems.

Comparative analysis as a method in politics is at least as old as Aristotle, but its self-conscious growth as a specialised area in the discipline can be dated from after the Second World War, when political scientists attempted to be more 'scientific', and to go beyond the limits of the institutional and legalistic description of western polities that had formed the staple of the discipline in the past. Works of deliberate comparison came to form the core of this sub-area, whether concerned with total political systems and their formal institutions (generally the concern of comparative government) or with informal institutions, political functions, ideologies, processes and political cultures (which, together with comparative government, can be called comparative politics). Examples of these works include: M. Duverger, *Political Parties*, Methuen, rev. edn, 1959; L. Epstein, *Political Parties in Western Democracies*, Pall Mall, 1967; B. Chapman, *The Profession of Government*, Allen & Unwin, 1959; M. Ameller, ed., *Parliaments*, Cassell, rev. edn, 1966; and the Princeton series on political development. In addition, several works on methodology have been written, notably: G. Hecksher, *The Study of Comparative Government and Politics*, Allen & Unwin, 1957, and R. Macridis, *The Study of Comparative Government*, New York, Random House, 1955.

Several major methodological problems have been identified. First, comparison itself presupposes a conceptual framework or initial classificatory scheme, according to which the selection and rejection of items for comparison can be undertaken. Yet one of the purposes of comparative analysis is to discover new relationships and classifications, so any initial scheme of classification has to be tentative, and capable of modification. The level of comparison is another problem; too general a level may well lead to the omission of significant detail and the production of broad, but unilluminating, generalisations. Yet comparison conducted at too specific a level may be overdetailed and provide generalisations which are too narrow in scope to be useful. Problems of language, of the validity of comparisons of apparently similar components or processes from different cultures, of the availability of data, also complicate comparative analysis.

☞ COMPARATIVE GOVERNMENT; COMPARATIVE POLITICS; ETHNOCENTRISM; POLITICAL ANALYSIS

Comparative government

Though often used (e.g. as the title of an academic course or a textbook) interchangeably with the term 'comparative politics', comparative government may be usefully distinguished as the study of states and their governmental institutions and processes, on a comparative basis. Such usage is defended by those political scientists who distinguish the state as a political organisation from lesser political communities (see J. Blondel, *An Introduction to Comparative Government*, Weidenfeld & Nicolson, 1969, ch. 1).

Thus the comparison of regimes (as conducted e.g. by Aristotle) and their stages of development (see e.g. G. Field, *Comparative Political Development*, Routledge, 1968), of legislatures, executives and judicial bodies and their functions, of systems of local government and devolution, of constitutions, and perhaps also of the political collectivities—parties and pressure groups—that seek to use or influence political power at the state level, as well as systems of election, of leadership selection and succession, of revolutions and civil war, all would fall within the scope of comparative government.

Examples of works of comparative government analysis are given in the entry on COMPARATIVE ANALYSIS above. In addition reference should be made to the several readers mentioned in the entry on COMPARATIVE POLITICS below, and to the very useful source of comparative data by A. Banks and R. Textor, eds., *A Cross-Polity Survey*, Massachusetts Institute of Technology Press, 1963.

☛ COMPARATIVE ANALYSIS; COMPARATIVE POLITICS; GOVERNMENT (B): study area

Comparative politics

Though often used interchangeably with the term 'comparative government' to describe comparative studies in political science, 'comparative politics' can usefully be distinguished from that term as being a wider and more inclusive area of study. Not only is it concerned with the comparative study of the state and its institutions and processes, but it also includes in its field the wider range of political structures, functions and values found in both state and non-state political contexts, such as leadership, political socialisation, the resolution of political conflict, bargaining, decision-making in political institutions, and political communication.

A useful survey of such subjects is to be found in G. Almond and G. Powell, *Comparative Politics: a Developmental Approach*, Little, Brown, 1966, and in the companion volumes of country and analytical studies in that series. The field is also sampled thoroughly in two readers: H. Eckstein and D. Apter, eds., *Comparative Politics*, New York, Free Press, 1963, and R. Macridis and B. Brown, eds., *Comparative Politics*, Homewood, USA, Dorsey Press, rev. edn, 1964.

☛ COMPARATIVE ANALYSIS; COMPARATIVE GOVERNMENT

Component

Any item which is an identifiable part of a system, i.e. a system is composed of interrelated components. In a political system, political actors, structures and institutions are all components.

☛ POLITICAL SYSTEM

Computer utilisation

Computers may be used in several fields of political science, particularly where complicated mathematical or other data-processing operations are involved. Their development since the 1950s has enabled the emphasis on quantification, simulation and model-building in the social sciences to proceed at a faster rate than would otherwise have been possible.

The major uses by political scientists of computers have been: for mathematical calculations, where computers can perform complicated operations swiftly and accurately (e.g. for certain types of factor analysis, content analysis, or the calculation and analysis of election results, as occurred in West Germany after the votes had been cast in the 1969 election); for the storage and retrieval of information (e.g. the various survey data banks at the Universities of Michigan, Köln, Essex, etc.; comparative surveys of states such as the 'Cross-Polity Survey'); for high-speed simulations, man-machine gaming, etc. (e.g. the Simulmatics operation for Kennedy's 1960 campaign, and various academic 'games' that have been developed using conflict scenarios); as analogies for the development of models of political processes (Karl Deutsch's communications model is a major example).

It must be remembered that computer time is still a costly

resource; that the output of a computer can only be as useful as the input is accurate and relevant; and that quantification itself in political science is still in its infancy.

Many of the opportunities and problems of computer utilisation are surveyed in D. Bobrow and J. Schwartz, eds., *Computers and the Policy-Making Community*, Prentice-Hall, 1968.

☛ GAMING; MATHEMATICAL ANALYSIS; SIMULATION

Concept

A concept is the meaning conveyed by some word which represents an idea, and which is capable of forming its own category of objects, phenomena, processes, etc., e.g. the concepts of class, interest, power, in politics.

Concepts are the elements from which complex statements are constructed about relationships, and which go to form their explanation, thus a theory or scientific law will consist of several interrelated concepts.

☛ CONCEPTUAL FRAMEWORK; THEORY

Conceptual framework

A set of concepts, some of which may be in the form of hypotheses and theories, which constitutes a classificatory scheme for the explanation and analysis of certain types of phenomena. In political science, the Marxian theories of historical determinism and social class, the functionalist ideas of Talcott Parsons, the concepts and models of game theory and the communications approach of Deutsch are all examples of conceptual frameworks.

☛ CONCEPT; MODEL

Concurrent majority

A majority composed of several distinct elements or interests, whose agreement to a proposal is regarded as a necessary political requirement for its implementation, though legally a simple majority may suffice.

☛ CONSENSUS; MAJORITY; VETO GROUP

Confederation

A form of government of a territorial area, in which several previously autonomous states agree to vest certain defined and limited powers (e.g. concerning trade or defence) in a new collective authority, while retaining their separate identity and their independence with regard to all powers not so vested.

Though territorial contiguity is not essential to the formation of a confederation, it is often vital to its successful continuation.

Confederations may persist, may disintegrate, or may develop into federations.

Examples of confederations: the states of North America from the creation of the Articles of Confederation to the coming into force of the Federal Constitution (1781–89), the Southern Confederacy in the US civil war, and various confederations in Germany during the nineteenth century.

☛ AUTONOMY; FEDERATION

Confessional parties

Political parties, such as the Christian Democrats in Italy, or several of the parties in Lebanese politics, who recognise a more or less formal relationship between their party principles and the religious principles of some creed or denomination, e.g. the Catholic faith, Buddhism. The opposite of a confessional party is a secular party, where no such formal relationship is recognised, e.g. the major parties of Britain and the USA, the Social Democrats in West Germany.

☛ CHRISTIAN DEMOCRACY; PARTY

Conflict approach

A conflict approach to political analysis is one that focuses on the political behaviour of individuals and groups in terms of the competition between them for the values which are distributed by political means, the processes by which conflicts—over policies, priorities, methods of attaining goals or selecting leaders—are resolved, and the effects of conflict on the structures of the political system. In the case of international politics, where conflict has been a major concept in study and research, the relations between state political systems can be examined in large part in terms of conflict approaches.

Such approaches include the use of formal models, such as game theory, various mathematical techniques where the variables of the conflict situation can be quantified, bargaining theory, the study of communication, techniques such as gaming and simulation, etc., and several of these are examined in K. Boulding, *Conflict and Defense: a general theory*, Harper & Row, 1962. Also of interest as an analytical examination of political conflict is A. Rapoport, *Fights, Games and Debates*, Michigan University Press, 1960.

☛ BARGAINING THEORY; GAME THEORY; POLITICAL SYSTEM; POLITICS; SIMULATION

Consensus

Consensus is a state of agreement or acceptance concerning matters of importance; in political contexts, therefore, consensus is agreement about matters such as the goals of a political system, its methods of attaining them, its procedures for decision-making and the resolution of conflict, and its methods of selection of the occupants of political roles. Consensus, being a matter of degree, may vary on each of these matters within a system over time, and there need be no congruence between the extent of consensus over e.g. system goals, and that over decision-making procedures or leadership selection methods.

Consensus reflects, then, the degree of sharing of values and the acceptance of norms in a political community, and is related, in the systems model of Easton, for example, to the inputs of *support* into the political system. In turn, it is affected by the performance of the system. The degree of consensus may be related to the degree of homogeneity in a society; it may be difficult to preserve high levels of homogeneity in a pluralist society, or in a society in which subsystem factors are politically of great relevance, e.g. religious, regional or ethnic identities. Political integration thus depends on the existence of minimum levels of consensus over goals, procedures, methods and political authority.

☛ ALIENATION; CLEAVAGE; COHESION; POLITICAL INTEGRATION; SUPPORT

Conservatism

A set of beliefs deriving from a view of society as complex and organic, rather than functional and mechanistic. This view implies a distrust of political change, especially of a sudden, violent or radical nature, as being more likely to damage than to improve the delicate interrelationships of society; instead, reliance is placed on a maintenance of traditional institutions and processes, even when apparently these are outmoded and irrational, which may be modified only with extreme caution and to meet present needs rather than some future design; renovation, rather than reconstruction, of the social fabric.

Certain political consequences stem from these beliefs. The idea that society is complex and organic leads to a protective attitude to the multiple groups that constitute society, and to a suspicion of state interference, centralisation, bureaucratic structures and the extension of state control through the undertaking of new social tasks. Conservatives tend to be sympathetic towards property rights, and to accept that the inequalities within society reflected in class divisions, educational and status differentials, etc., and the distribution of wealth and property should all be recognised as requiring a political order based on hierarchy.

Conservatism in these terms is often found as the ideological foundation of conservative political parties, e.g. the Conservative Party in Great Britain, the Gaullist Party in France, and is an important ideological current within the Republican Party of the USA. It is often contrasted with liberalism, but conservatism is more precisely an antonym of radicalism, as many conservatives would find several aspects of liberalism not uncongenial.

☛ HIERARCHY; IDEOLOGY; LIBERALISM; RADICALISM

Conspiracy

A group of persons linked by their joint plan to accomplish some illegal purpose. A political conspiracy is thus aimed at achieving some unconstitutional and illegal end, such as the overthrow of a government or the manipulation of an election. The legal definition of conspiracy, varying from state to state, may be wider than the normal usage of the word in political contexts.

☛ COUP D'ÉTAT; PUTSCH

Conspiracy theories

Belief systems which include the notion that certain social phenomena of importance, particularly those considered to be harmful or evil, are the result of a conspiracy among certain members of society, often regarded as agents of a foreign power. People who hold such theories usually possess evidence, in which they believe unquestioningly, concerning the people and the strategies involved in the conspiracy, and often regard it as their obligation to expose and defeat the plot that they have uncovered.

Many examples have existed of widespread conspiracy theories (e.g. anti-Catholicism, Populism in some of its forms), but anti-Semitism in its modern form (e.g. as based on the *Protocols of the Elders of Zion*) and anti-Communism in the United States (e.g. the 'witch-hunting' of Senator Joe McCarthy) are two of the more important in terms of their social effects.

☞ ANTI-SEMITISM; POPULISM

Constituency

A group of voters (the constituents) entitled to elect a representative or delegate. It is thus usually a territorial area, but in some political bodies the constituency may be a functional or other grouping, such as a member union within a confederation of trade unions, or the employers on an industrial negotiating committee.

A secondary usage is to refer to the group or section of society from which a politician derives his influence, independent of any formal electoral arrangements, e.g. a spokesman for the military in an autocratic regime.

Constitution

A fundamental statement of laws governing the citizen's political rights, the political institutions, their functions and their relationships, within a particular political community. In most cases it is in written form, though the United Kingdom is said to possess an 'unwritten' constitution.

Constitutions may be created by many means, including the use of constitutional conventions, imposition by an external power, an Act of the legislature, or the confirmation of a document by a referendum. They may legitimately be altered usually only by the processes laid down in the Constitution itself, and often these are complicated and difficult, though in an unwritten constitution such alteration is much simpler.

In many countries, there is a process of judicial review which can void any law or action of the government, or of other groups or individuals, which conflicts with the judges' interpretation of the constitution.

☛ CONSTITUTIONAL LAW; CONVENTION (A): the
  institution; CONVENTION (B): procedural conventions;
  GOVERNMENT (A): the institution; JUDICIAL REVIEW

Constitutional law

The rules and procedures concerning the relationships among the structures of government, and their principal powers and functions. In political communities possessing a written constitution, this will be a primary source of constitutional law, while in all states a major source will be the decisions of the courts of law which interpret such rules.

In Britain the study of constitutional law includes the general principles of constitutional doctrine such as parliamentary supremacy and the rule of law (Britain lacks a written formal constitution); the law, conventions and procedural rules relating to Parliament, including its election and its functions; the powers of the monarch and the executive branch, including the control and limitation of those powers; the role of the judiciary in relation to constitutional matters; the rights and duties of the citizen relating to the government. In America the subject would include the study of the constitution and the interpretations of its wording in the form of legal decisions; the federal relationship; and the functions and powers of the President, the Executive and Congress.

☛ ADMINISTRATIVE LAW; CONSTITUTION; JUDICIAL
  REVIEW; RULE OF LAW

Constitutionalism

The term has two related meanings: one concerning constitutionalism as practice, the other as the positive valuation of that practice.

Constitutionalism as practice is the ordering of political processes and institutions on the basis of a constitution, which lays down the pattern of formal political institutions and embodies the basic political norms of a society. The constitution not only regulates the relationships of organs of government to each other; it also limits the discretionary powers of government, and, in doing so, protects the citizen. Such regulation and limitation require arbitration by some judicial body (e.g. in the USA and the German Federal Republic, by 'supreme' or constitutional courts which apply judicial review to governmental acts; in Britain by the ordinary system of courts and civil and criminal remedies), as well as enforcement. Thus while the USSR, for example, possesses a constitution, neither the specific machinery for its enforcement nor the acceptance of its constraints by the political authorities is much in evidence. Though not found only in democratic regimes, constitutionalism is a basic requirement of a democracy.

As a term of valuation, constitutionalism refers to the ideas of those who wish to preserve, or introduce, the political supremacy of a constitution within a particular state, to act as a protector of the citizen from arbitrary government and as a statement of political relationships, especially where these do not exist already in satisfactory form. Stress is laid on the 'rule of law' as a fundamental concept from which constitutionalism derives.

☛ CONSTITUTION; RULE OF LAW

Constraint

In political analysis, a constraint is any factor which sets limits to the possible alternative forms of behaviour (of a political actor, a component of a system, or of the system itself) that might otherwise exist. Constraints are thus contextual: they exist only in relation to a given situation. Among the major classes of constraints are: time; limitation of resources; the capacity of communication channels; the actions and decisions of other actors and systems.

☛ SYSTEMS ANALYSIS

Content analysis

A technique used in the social sciences to classify and measure characteristics in an item of communication, according to an objective set of preselected categories. The unit of measurement may be e.g. the word, the sentence or the theme.

Examples of its use in political analysis include measurement of variations in themes expressed in nomination acceptance speeches of US presidential candidates; the analysis of propaganda; and measurement of changes in Sino-Soviet relations, as expressed in their publications, according to the level of international tension.

A useful introductory guide to content analysis is O. Holsti,

Content Analysis for the Social Sciences and Humanities, USA, Addison-Wesley, 1969.

☛ COMPUTER UTILISATION; POLITICAL
  COMMUNICATION

Contract theory

A theory concerning the logical and legal—though not the historical—basis of the state as a political community, associated with the writings of many philosophers from the early Greeks onwards, but finding particularly coherent expression in the writings of Locke and Rousseau.

This theory, in its simplest form, holds that a state is an organisation which should be regarded as having been formed by a 'social contract', a contract in which each member gives up certain of his rights associated with his 'freedom in the state of nature', in return for every other member equally abandoning such rights. By extension, this contract holds for each new member of the state. As a form of historical, rather than philosophical or legal and logical, explanation of the existence and competence of the state, it is lacking in foundation, except in rare cases such as the 'Mayflower Compact', or, less precisely, the signing of new constitutions, e.g. for the USA in 1787, or for West Germany in 1949.

Some uses of the contract theory apply to the political relationship between ruler and ruled, e.g. the notion that obedience is given to a ruler only so long as his commands are in accordance with some external standard, such as the law, 'natural law', a constitution, the precepts of Christianity, custom, etc. Rebellion is justified, on these terms, if this contract is broken by the ruler.

A general survey of the development of contract theory is J. Gough, *The Social Contract*, Oxford University Press, 1957.

☛ STATE

Conurbation

An area of densely populated territory of a predominantly urban type, produced by the outward growth of several neighbouring towns or cities. Politically, it consists of several separate local authorities, though reform of local government arrangements may provide for a conurbation which has a single local government authority, or which is included in a wider regional authority.

In Britain, the Registrars-General recognise seven conurbations for demographic purposes: Greater London; Merseyside; South East Lancashire; West Yorkshire; West Midlands; Tyneside; Central Clydeside. With the exception of Tyneside (about 850,000) each had a population in 1968 in excess of one million.

☛ CITY; LOCAL GOVERNMENT STUDIES; METROPOLIS; URBAN STUDIES

Convention (A): the institution

Meetings of political groups for various purposes are sometimes termed 'conventions' when they are formally 'convened' for a stated aim. Two major types of conventions are: constitutional conventions, where delegates or representatives meet to formulate a new national or provincial constitution, e.g. in the USA in 1787, in Germany in 1919 (the Weimar Constitution) and in the German Federal Republic in 1948–49 (the Bonn Constitution); and nominating conventions, as held by the major political parties in the USA, to select the party nominees for e.g. the presidential and vice-presidential elections, and to draft a platform for them to put forward as policy proposals.

☛ CONSTITUTION; CONVENTION (B): procedural conventions

Convention (B): procedural conventions

Rules which state certain norms or procedures to regulate political relationships, but which, if breached, do not involve the application of legal sanctions.

Conventions are usually unwritten, though some preambles to statutes or written constitutions—to which courts of law will refuse to give recognition—may be considered to be conventional statements.

Conventions arise to give guidance as to conduct where formal rules are silent or ambiguous. Generally they develop from precedents, but may be matters of agreement between political actors. They may be changed as circumstances change, but if breached may well give rise to a political crisis, or to the need for a more specific legal rule to govern such cases in the future. However, because they are often unwritten, their precise content is often a matter of interpretation, which may itself lead to dispute.

Examples of conventions: in the United Kingdom, the power of the prime minister to choose the date of dissolution of Parliament, subject to the five-year limit imposed by the Parliament Act 1911, and the duty of a minister in the Cabinet to abide by decisions of the Cabinet or to resign; in the United States, the convention of the party loyalty of presidential electors chosen by the people to elect the President in the Electoral College, and the very existence as well as the membership of the President's Cabinet; there appears to be a convention of allowing an incumbent President the second term permitted to him under the Basic Law in the German Federal Republic.

The word 'convention' is also used to refer to agreements between states which have a treaty-like form, e.g. the European Convention on Human Rights, and the Geneva Conventions on the rules of warfare.

☛ CONVENTION (A): the institution; CUSTOM; TREATY

Conversion process

A term applied in input-output analysis based on the idea of the political system, to indicate the changing of one type of input into another, or into an output, In the exposition of the analysis of political systems associated with David Easton, wants (e.g. preferences, opinions) are converted into demands, and demands in turn may be converted into issues, which undergo processing by the authorities, either to result in outputs (such as decisions and policies), or to disappear from the attention of the authorities (e.g. due to changing circumstances). See chapters 5–7 in David Easton, *A Systems Analysis of Political Life*, Wiley, 1965, for a discussion of the conversion process.

A less technical usage is to refer to the process by which a person is induced to change his opinions, attitudes or allegiance on some matter (e.g. 'he was converted to socialism by his experiences in the General Strike').

☛ AGGREGATION; INPUT-OUTPUT ANALYSIS; POLITICAL SYSTEM; SYSTEMS ANALYSIS

Correlation

Correlation refers to a degree of correspondence or common variation in independent measurements of two different items, e.g. age and size of majority in the case of legislators. It is measured by the coefficient of correlation (expressed as *r*) which ranges from +1.0 (complete positive correlation) to −1.0 (complete negative or inverse correlation). A coefficient of correlation of zero indicates that there is no co-variance or correspondence in the two items measured. In the example given above, a survey might reveal a coefficient of correlation of +0.85, between age and size of majority expressed in percentage terms, indicating a high degree of correspondence.

☛ STATISTICAL ANALYSIS; VARIABLES

Corruption

Corruption, in a political context, is any act of employing political roles or offices for illegal or unethical purposes, but particularly when some element of personal advantage (especially of a financial nature) is present. Examples of corruption in the past have included bribery of voters by candidates, voters demanding payment for their vote from candidates, improper use of political information for personal gain, and partiality in the leasing of government property (e.g. the Teapot Dome scandal in the USA, 1921–22).

☛ NEPOTISM

Country studies

Studies of political behaviour, institutions and processes which focus on a particular country, and which attempt to identify and analyse the relevant political factors within that country, including often the effects of the economic and other social subsystems on the political subsystem. Lord Bryce's *The American Commonwealth* (1888) is an early and classic example.

Coup d'état

A change of regime brought about by illegal and unconstitutional action on the part of a holder, or group of holders, of some political (including military) office. It often involves violence, though generally limited in its extent. It may be preceded by a conspiracy concerned with obtaining certain political offices for sympathisers (a key ministry, a strategic military command, or control of important communications facilities).

C 54

It is similar to a revolution in so far as its purpose involves a sudden and illegal change of regime; it differs from it in that it does not call on mass support to effect such changes, though it may seek legitimation of the changes by a plebiscite or mass demonstration. A putsch is a form of coup d'état.

Examples of coups include the initiation of imperial regimes by Napoleon I and Louis Napoleon; Cromwell's seizure of power in England; the Nigerian military coup in 1966–67; the change of government in Bolivia in 1969; the Cambodian coup in 1970.

☞ PLEBISCITE; PUTSCH; REGIME; PALACE REVOLUTION; REVOLUTION

Crisis

A condition of extreme instability. Thus, in a political context, the time when elements of a political system are in an unstable state, and liable to change their relationships to each other and to the system, or their own state. Thus a controversial policy proposal, an external threat to the security of the system, a decline in political resources, a challenge to the legitimacy of the political authorities may all constitute a political crisis.

A crisis need not lead to change; it can be overcome and the situation return to its former state.

Critical range

A concept employed in systems approaches to political analysis, which refers to the range of levels within which, if persisted in for some period of time, stress on the components of the system is dangerous for the functioning or the persistence of the system itself, or for certain of its subsystems. For example, a diminution in support for the system may reach such a critical range, and, if some corrective action (or 'response') does not follow, may result in the disintegration of the system.

☞ ADAPTATION; RESPONSE; STRESS; SYSTEMS ANALYSIS

Cross-sectional analysis

Analysis by means of the employment of comparisons at the same point of time of several areas or cases representing different stages of development of the factor under investigation, e.g. political awareness of a child, an adolescent, an adult of working age, and a retired adult.

☛ COHORT ANALYSIS; LONGITUDINAL ANALYSIS

Cube law

A law which sets out a mathematical relationship between the share of the seats in the legislature which a political party will obtain, and the proportion of the vote which it receives, provided that (*a*) there is a system of simple majority voting, and (*b*) that only two parties are in contention.

Where two parties, A and B, contest the election, the law predicts that if the votes are divided in a ratio of $X:Y$, seats won will be in the ratio of $X^3:Y^3$.

D. Butler (*The Electoral System in Britain since 1918*, Oxford University Press, 2nd edn, 1963) stresses that the law can only be expected to apply in a relatively homogeneous political culture, with equal-sized constituencies.

☛ PSEPHOLOGY

Custom

A habitual action or set of actions within a specific social situation, which may or may not be directly related to the overt or 'manifest' functions of the institution or group within which it occurs.

In politics, it is sometimes distinguished from 'convention' on the grounds that conventions can be seen to have some part to play in the preservation or development of the functions of an institution (e.g. the British Cabinet, the American Senate, the German Chancellorship), whereas customs can be regarded as mere embodiments of the culture or tradition of the institution, capable of abolition or amendment without necessarily harming the functional efficiency of the institution.

Examples of political customs: the concession of the election by a defeated presidential candidate before all the results are known; 'Black Rod' and other procedures involved in the opening of Parliament; the sentiments of gratitude to the Returning Officer expressed by candidates on the declaration of the poll at a British general election.

☛ CONVENTION (B): procedural conventions; NORM

D

Decentralisation

A dispersion of power among several entities or units within a political system, or the process of such dispersion. A federal state such as the USA, Canada or West Germany, is usually by definition a decentralised state; unitary states such as France and Great Britain are relatively centralised.

☛ CENTRALISATION; DEVOLUTION; FEDERATION; REGIONALISM

Decision

A decision is a choice of goals, or means of attaining some goal, from among those seen to be available as alternatives at the time, for the purpose of responding to the requirements of a particular complex situation, or some situation thought likely to occur in the future.

The range of alternatives seen to be available will be circumscribed by various constraints, from the environment and from within the decision-making structure itself. The rules and procedures governing the process of decision-making will also be important factors affecting the choice of a decision.

In politics, decisions are made in the form of policies, votes—

both for candidates for office and for substantive or procedural proposals, implementing or executive decisions, and organisational or procedural decisions.

☛ CONSTRAINT; DECISION-MAKING ANALYSIS; POLICY; VOTING

Decision-making analysis

The analysis of political systems, processes and behaviour in terms of the political decisions which are made, including the structures involved in decision-making, the factors influencing the outcomes of the process, and the political costs of decisions, as well as the selection of actors for decision-making roles.

Though sometimes used synonymously with policy analysis, decision-making analysis is distinguished both by its concern with decisions that are not in themselves policies (e.g. with voting decisions), or which are only part of a wider-ranging policy process, and by its concentration of attention on the political factors involved in decision-making, whereas policy analysis concerns itself with a more extensive range of factors, as well as with processes that precede and follow the decision stage in policy-making, e.g. with implementation.

Among the approaches to decision-making analysis that have been employed are: game theory, with its emphasis on the quantification of the results of decision strategies in certain types of competitive situation; approaches derived from economics, including notions of maximising advantage from decisions, indifference curve analysis, and the analogies between economic and political decision-making; the creation of decision models and the identification of variables or stages involved in the decision-making process, as in the work of Snyder and Lasswell.

Major studies have drawn on contributions from many other disciplines, including psychology, sociology, administrative theory and organisation theory. As well as several case studies of decisions and decision-makers, some of them based on laboratory simulations, there have been studies of the social and economic background of decision-makers; the role of communications in decision-making; decision-making in local and international, as well as in state, politics; the relationships between institutional structures and styles of decision-making; and a wide range of studies on various types of voting decisions. A survey of many aspects of decision-making analysis can be found in an essay by R. Snyder, 'A decision-making approach to the study of political phenomena', in R. Young, ed., *Approaches to the Study of Politics*, Evanston, USA, Northwestern University Press, 1958.

Attempts have been made to relate the findings of political decision-making analysis to the work on decisions carried out by other social scientists, such as economists and sociologists, in an effort to produce a set of generalised concepts and hypotheses, but these are still very much in the exploratory stage.

☛ COMMUNITY STUDIES; DECISION; ECONOMIC APPROACHES TO POLITICS; POLICY; POLICY ANALYSIS; POLICY APPROACH; PSEPHOLOGY; SMALL GROUP POLITICS

Definition

A statement by which the distinctive meaning of a word, phrase or sign is conveyed. Definitions may be created by referring to the uses of the term in its various contexts, and then stating the meaning the word possesses in such contexts. Definitions may be 'stipulative', i.e. they may state in advance that when terms are used they will be intended to convey the meanings that are stipulated in the definition; they may be taxonomic, in which case the terms are stated with regard to certain features or properties that make up some classification, e.g. as with botanical definitions; or they may be operational, where the definition of a term states certain operations, such as measurement, which, if carried out as specified, will distinguish whether or not an object falls within the terms of the definition, e.g. the meteorological definition of a gale-force wind.

☛ OPERATIONALISATION

Delegate

A person chosen to act on behalf of a group in some context where the whole group cannot be present, such as a conference or a convention. Such activity may include voting in accordance with previous decisions of the group, presenting the group's viewpoint in debate, or bargaining on its behalf.

As Burke pointed out in his speech to the electors of Bristol, a delegate is in a different position to that of a representative. A delegate may only act within a limited sphere, designated in advance, and may be bound in advance to speak or vote in ways predetermined by the delegating authority. A representative, on the other hand, is expected to use his personal judgment.

☞ DELEGATION; PROXY; REPRESENTATION

Delegated legislation

Legislation, or rules which have the force of legislation, made by a subordinate individual or body under powers delegated to it by a superior institution. Thus, in a state, ministers or agencies may have legislative powers delegated to them by Parliament, Congress or some similar legislative assembly. Such legislation as is made under delegated powers is usually subject to scrutiny, at least potentially, by the parent legislature, and is capable of being nullified by a decision of that body.

The purposes of delegated legislative powers are manifold, but in particular they save the time and the energy of members of the legislature, enable specialised legislation to be drawn up by experts, and allow greater speed and flexibility in the making of rules regarding e.g. emergency situations.

☞ DEVOLUTION; EMERGENCY LAWS; LEGISLATURE; REGULATION (B): rule

Delegation

The transference, usually under strict limiting conditions, of power or authority from some person or group to some other, usually subordinate, person or group.

Examples of political delegation: a trade union branch to its delegates to the annual conference; Parliament to a ministerial department; a foreign ministry to a delegate at an international conference.

☞ DELEGATED LEGISLATION

Delphi method

A method of utilising the opinions of experts to arrive at informed forecasts for purposes of planning or prediction. It is based on a carefully scheduled series of questionnaires, reports and information-feedback, generally conducted through the mail. Usually a problem is stated, and several related questions drawn up, which each expert is asked to consider before responding. The results of the initial enquiry are aggregated, and returned to the experts who are asked either to justify their own forecasts if these are significantly different from the median or mean, or to modify them. This process may be repeated, with new questions added if necessary. The results may then be considered an informed consensus, if the panel of experts was well selected initially, and if the questions are framed suitably.

☛ PLANNING; PREDICTION

Demagogue

A political leader, often of a charismatic type, who seeks to win or retain power by the use of emotive claims and charges regarding his policies and the dangers of his opponents' policies. These claims and charges are directed at what he believes to be popular opinions and prejudices, and they are made heedless of the facts of the situation.

Leaders who may be said to have employed demagogic methods in the past include Hitler, Goebbels, Senator Joseph McCarthy and Benito Mussolini.

☛ CHARISMA; LEADERSHIP; PROPAGANDA

Democracy

A form of rule in which either the members of a society act as the policy-making authority (direct democracy) or are represented by a smaller number to make policy on their behalf (representative democracy).

Historically, the typical examples of direct democracy have been the fourth-century BC Athenian, and seventeenth- and eighteenth-century New England 'town meeting' models. In these cases the citizenry, still in numbers small enough to offer the opportunities of individual participation, met periodically to discuss issues, receive reports from executive officials, and take decisions. The growth in size of the populations of cities and states, the distances they cover, and the vast, complex and continuous stream of issues requiring governmental consideration, decision and action, plus the inability of a population to devote much time to political participation, set limits to the extension of direct democracy; where popular participation was regarded as desirable, it had to be through the election of representatives and perhaps through the use of occasional referenda and plebiscites.

Democracy implies certain operational principles for its realisation. Participation must be equal: every vote in a democracy should count for the same as every other vote. In representative democracy this raises questions concerning the apportionment of electoral districts, the type of electoral system used, and the rules governing electoral procedures. The principle of majority decision of substantive issues must be accepted (though special majorities may be required for procedural alterations, e.g. constitutional amendments), for this is the only salient method of settling disputes by voting rather than by compromise procedures. The possible effects of 'improper' influence on the voter should be minimised, thus secret ballots, limitations on electoral expenditure and laws regarding mass media communications during the period of an election are all relevant. The principles of protection of minority rights or of civil liberties, and the rule of law, are generally also associated with democracy as a concept, though logically they are not essential to its basic definition.

Because any actual political system will contain imperfections in relation to the operational principles outlined here, due to the development of political parties, interest groups and other intermediary organisations, and the fact that the values held by some members of a democracy may be regarded by them as being of more importance than the preservation of democracy as a form of rule, the application of the term to any existing state will always be liable to criticism. Conversely, the term may be claimed as descriptive of the form of rule of even totalitarian Communist states, on the grounds that the changes of economic relationships only found in Communist society are an essential prerequisite of equal participation in politics of all citizens. Thus as an actual classificatory category it is less efficient than some form of typology of rule based on e.g. the number of political parties, type of electoral system or form of legislative-executive relations.

☛ ARISTOCRACY; AUTOCRACY; DICTATORSHIP; MAJORITY; OLIGARCHY; PARTICIPATION; POPULISM; REPRESENTATION; RULE OF LAW; TOTALITARIANISM

Demography

The study of the statistical aspects of human population, including especially the analysis of the numbers and distribution of population in a specified territorial area; changes in the characteristics of populations over time; the age and sex compositions of populations; their marital, occupational and other relevant social characteristics; the size of family units; birth, death and migration rates. From such studies demographers have developed interests in the economic, social and political causes and effects of changes in the characteristics of populations, and have developed a range of special mathematical techniques for analysing their data.

☛ POPULATION

Depoliticisation

☞ POLITICISATION

Depth interview

An interview which seeks to obtain information concerning attitudes, opinions and beliefs, conducted usually on the basis of a flexible questionnaire which permits open-ended questions to be supplemented by spontaneous additional questions as necessary, and where a particular matter can be dealt with in considerable detail, probing deeply into the subject under investigation—hence the term 'depth' interview.

Depth interviews may be single, or in series, as necessary. As they are often concerned with psychological aspects of e.g. political attitudes and behaviour, and as often the exact wording, even the hesitancies and repetitions used, becomes important, it is not unusual to record the interviews on tape, for later reference and transcription. All these aspects: the detail and flexibility of the questionnaire, the necessary skills of the interviewer, recording and transcription, make for high costs per interview compared to standard questionnaire-based surveys. The time taken up in arranging, conducting and reviewing each interview is also a major administrative factor inhibiting its use as a technique.

As an example, part of the methodology of the study of *The Authoritarian Personality* (Harper & Row, 1950), by Adorno and his colleagues, involved the use of depth interviews.

☛ INTERVIEW; SURVEY

Determinism

The belief that some set of effects can be sufficiently explained by reference to a limited set of laws or causes, and that other causes of these effects are either irrelevant or are secondary to the primary 'determining' set. Thus Marxism is often held to be a theory based on economic determinism—in this case that political and social relationships are determined by underlying patterns of economic forces, especially those of the ownership of the means of production. Other forms of determinism have centred around race, religion, personality and culture.

The major criticism of determinist explanations is that they rule out in advance the possibility of multiple causation.

Determinist theories

☞ DETERMINISM

Development studies

Development studies are interdisciplinary and multidisciplinary investigations of development in so-called underdeveloped or developing societies. Such studies generally accept the view that development is a multidimensional phenomenon, in which economic, political, demographic, social, technological and cultural factors all interact. They may be focused on a country, area or region; often they will be problem oriented (concentrating on such topics as planning, communications, technical education, political stability), though some development studies are primarily methodological or descriptive in orientation.

Examples of multidisciplinary development studies are: R. Asher *et al.*, *Development of the Emerging Countries: an agenda for research*, Brookings Institution, Washington, 1962; C. Geertz, ed., *Old Societies and New States*, New York, Free Press, 1963; A. Waterston, *Development Planning: lessons of experience*, Oxford University Press, 1966.

☛ MODERNISATION; POLITICAL DEVELOPMENT

Devolution

The delegation of specific powers to some subordinate unit of government, e.g. control of certain functions of government by Northern Ireland, Scotland and Wales through grant of powers by the United Kingdom Parliament. It is thus more limited and specific a term than decentralisation.

☛ DECENTRALISATION; DELEGATION; REGIONALISM

d'Hondt method

The d'Hondt method is a way of calculating how seats in a legislature (or other elective offices) should be distributed among candidates from party lists in a system of proportional representation. It is named after its inventor, Victor d'Hondt. West Germany is the best-known of the states that employ this method for their national elections.

When the election is completed and total votes per party list are known, these totals are successively divided by 1, 2, 3, . . . etc. These quotients are then ranked in order, with the name of the party list by each quotient. The number of seats available then determines how far down the list of quotients one goes in declaring candidates from party lists elected. As an example, assuming ten seats to be distributed among five party lists, and 120,000 valid votes cast as follows:

Party A	Party B	Party C	Party D	Party E
48,000	30,000	24,000	12,000	6,000

Then dividing by 2, 3, and 4 would give the following quotients:

24,000	15,000	12,000	6,000	3,000
16,000	10,000	8,000	4,000	2,000
12,000	7,500	6,000	3,000	1,500

The ten seats would therefore be distributed as follows:

Party A 4 seats (quotients of 48,000; 24,000; 16,000; 12,000)
Party B 3 seats (quotients of 30,000; 15,000; 10,000)
Party C 2 seats (quotients of 24,000; 12,000)
Party D 1 seat (quotient of 12,000)
Party E no seats.
If only five seats had been available, party A would have had three seats, and parties B and C one each.

This system of distribution may give different results at the margin from those given by some straight quota system (e.g. by dividing by a quota figure, and using 'greatest remainders' to distribute the last seats).

☞ ELECTORAL QUOTA; ELECTORAL SYSTEM; LIST SYSTEM; PROPORTIONAL REPRESENTATION

Dictatorship

A form of political rule in which power is concentrated in the hands of one man, or a small political clique. This power is often obtained by violent and unconstitutional means, and is exercised with little or no restraint from the judiciary or elected legislature, should they still be in existence. The rationale offered by the dictator for his assumption of power, for its continuation, for the violence and terror necessary to preserve his rule, and for the arbitrary and extensive exercise of governmental functions, is generally that the state is endangered by internal dissension or external enemies. Whether such is the case or not, such internal and external dangers are often the subject of propaganda disseminated by the dictator. Dictators also face problems of establishing their legitimacy, and may resort to the use of plebiscites, new constitutions, etc., for this purpose.

Constitutional dictators are those who assume emergency powers under legal and constitutional provisions, in time of crisis, and for limited periods. The dictatorship of the republican constitution of Rome and the powers contemplated under Article 48 of the Weimar Constitution of Germany were examples of this.

Non-constitutional dictators include: Julius Caesar, Oliver Cromwell, Franco, and the Greek 'Junta' which took power in April 1967.

☛ ABSOLUTISM; AUTOCRACY; LEADERSHIP;
   PLEBISCITE; TOTALITARIANISM

Direct action

Political activity which bypasses or ignores the constitutional channels which exist for the exercise of influence on policy-making, and which instead attempts either to directly change, or substitute for, that policy (e.g. 'squatters' occupying empty houses), or influence it by non-constitutional—though not necessarily illegal —means (e.g. strikes, embargoes on the handling of certain goods by dockers, disruption of public events).

Among recent examples of direct action have been various student protests in Britain, West Germany, France and the USA; antiwar protesters in America; the anti-apartheid protest movement during tours of Britain by South African sports teams.

☛ CIVIL DISOBEDIENCE

Direct democracy

Rule by the people of a state, town or other political community, by means of their direct participation in decision-making rather than through the election by them of representatives.

Direct democracy has been limited in the past to communities which have only relatively small numbers of citizens, since it was a necessary condition that they should be able to meet in one place. Thus it has been associated with e.g. Greek city-states, New England townships, British parish meetings, etc. However, modern communication techniques would, if it were desired, enable large numbers of citizens to vote directly on proposals in their own homes, by means of television, etc.

Devices such as the recall, the initiative and referenda have been used as limitations on representative democracy, and as compromises in favour of direct participation by citizens.

☛ DEMOCRACY; INITIATIVE; RECALL (A): the institution; REFERENDUM

Direct election

☞ ELECTION

Dissolution

The process by which the term of a legislature is brought to an end other than by completion of its maximum constitutional span. It is therefore generally applicable to the United Kingdom Parliament and to many Commonwealth legislatures, in certain special circumstances it could be applied to the West German *Bundestag*, but cannot be used in the USA where the term of Congress is fixed.

☛ LEGISLATURE

Droop quota

A method of calculating the electoral quota under a single transferable vote system. The quota (Q) is derived by dividing the total number of valid votes cast (V) by the number of seats to be filled (S) plus one, and adding one to the result. As a formula:

$$Q = \frac{V}{S+1} + 1.$$

☛ ELECTORAL QUOTA; SINGLE TRANSFERABLE VOTE SYSTEM

Due Process

Sometimes and more fully referred to as 'due process of law', this term refers to legal action which complies with procedural regulations and limitations laid down by a constitution, legislation or legal code, and the substantive content of which corresponds to vague ideas of fairness, the protection of individual rights and liberties, etc., which the judicial authorities are willing to recognise. It is primarily an Anglo-Saxon term.

☛ RULE OF LAW

Dynasty

The members of a family who rule a state in succession, usually as monarchs or emperors, e.g. the Hanoverian dynasty in Britain, the Napoleonic dynasty in France.

☛ MONARCHY

E

Eclectic approach

The approach to political analysis that rejects the view that any one system of ideas can be relied upon as a satisfactory explanatory method, and which therefore attempts to employ aspects of any system of explanation as seem best suited to the problem in hand.

☛ POLITICAL ANALYSIS

Economic approaches to politics

Economic approaches to politics are based on the assumptions that much of political activity and political behaviour is akin to economic activity and behaviour, and that the methods, models and concepts of the economist may be used with profit in the analysis of political processes.

The first assumption is based on those definitions of politics that focus on choice, decision-making, competition for 'goods', and the distribution of political resources. Elections, for example, are seen as market situations; political decision-making is seen as a process involving exchange; coalition formation and two-party political systems are regarded as equivalent in essential respects to oligopolistic and duopolistic market systems.

The second assumption draws attention to the range of concepts which the two disciplines share: resource allocation, demands, costs, utility, optimisation, etc. The cross-fertilisation by means of models, though mainly from economics to political science, is also noteworthy: input-output analysis, indifference analysis, game theory models, models of oligopolistic competition, etc.

Several scholars have produced books that set out to interpret a major portion of political life in terms of economic analysis. A. Downs, *An Economic Theory of Democracy*, Harper, 1957, considers the basic assumptions of democratic politics in terms of economic ideas. J. Buchanan and G. Tullock, *The Calculus of Consent*, University of Michigan Press, 1962, are concerned with formal problems of voting, coalitions, etc. R. Curry and L. Wade, *A Theory of Political Exchange*, Prentice-Hall, 1968, examine politics as a system of exchanges, involving decisions and decision-makers, in which the actors are concerned with maximising the benefits they receive and minimising the costs they incur. M. Olson, *The Logic of Collective Action*, Harvard University Press, 1965, deals with problems involved in the distribution of 'public goods', i.e. goods whose benefits are available to all members of a political public, but whose costs may be incurred only by some members.

☛ PARETO OPTIMUM; POLITICAL ECONOMY; POLITICAL RESOURCES

Election

The method for the selection of persons to fill certain offices by the votes of an electorate, i.e. of those qualified under the rules or procedures of the political system to express their choice from among the candidates available.

Elections are known as *direct* when the votes of the electorate are cast for candidates for office; the election is *indirect* if the electorate are only permitted to choose representatives or delegates, who in turn elect candidates to office. The American President is still elected indirectly, for instance, as was the President in the Fifth French Republic until the change in the Constitution in 1962.

Elections may also be divided into *single* and *multiple*. A single election occurs when only one candidate is elected to office in each constituency, as in the British or American elections to the legislature. A multiple election is one in which several offices are filled at the same time, as in the annual elections to the Labour Party National Executive.

All elections require an implicit or explicit set of rules and procedures to be known in advance.

☛ BALLOT; CANDIDATE; POLL; PSEPHOLOGY; VOTING

Electoral college

A body of electors with the responsibility of voting for some candidate for office, and themselves usually elected by a wider electorate, though in some electoral colleges members may be appointed ex-officio (e.g. the College of Cardinals who elect a new Pope). The President of the USA is still chosen by an electoral college, as was the President of the Fifth Republic in France, until the constitution was amended to permit popular election, in 1962.

☛ ELECTION

Electoral quota

Under electoral systems involving multi-member constituencies, based either on proportional representation or reallocation of votes according to preferences, the electoral quota is the number of votes that is required for a candidate to be elected.

Depending on the electoral system used, there are many methods of calculating quotas. For proportional representation systems involving party lists, the method of simple division of votes cast by the number of seats available can be used to set a quota (a party list with a quarter of the votes then gets a quarter of the seats), but this leaves a problem of marginal distributions where fractional remainders are involved. The d'Hondt system is a method by which the votes cast are divided by successive integers of the series 1, 2, 3, 4, . . . etc. Seats are allocated on the basis of the largest quotients resulting. The Saint-Laguë method is similar to the d'Hondt method, but the divisions are by integers of the series 1, 3, 5, etc., which tends to increase the proportions of seats going to the largest parties. For the single transferable vote system, the Droop quota is generally used, which divides the number of votes cast by the total number of seats plus one, adding one to the result to arrive at the quota necessary for election.

The calculation of the quota may be complicated, in proportional systems, by the imposition of a requirement that a party list must secure some minimum percentage of the vote before it qualifies for distributed seats (as in West Germany).

The term 'electoral quota' is also used to refer to the standard by which re-districting of constituencies is carried out, based usually on some average numbers of electors per seat.

☛ D'HONDT METHOD; DROOP QUOTA; ELECTORAL
SYSTEM; REAPPORTIONMENT

Electoral system

The institutional arrangements by means of which an election is conducted, and the purposes of the election fulfilled. Though many national electoral systems are as much the product of cultural factors as of some deliberate design, nevertheless they are usually capable of amendment, in order to meet the changes in what are held to be the proper functions of an election.

The main attributes of electoral systems, and which vary from system to system, are the designation of qualified electors; the territorial, functional or other basis of constituencies; the distribution of voting strength among the qualified electors; where other than simple plurality, single member districts are involved, the basis of representation and its calculation; the preliminary qualifications of candidates; the administrative arrangements of the election process itself including the rules concerning campaigning; the arrangements for receiving the results and for settling disputed results.

The major systems used in states for elections to the legislature are either direct election on the basis of a simple plurality from single-member districts, possibly involving a second ballot, or some form of proportional representation, such as the list system or multi-member constituencies.

☛ ALTERNATIVE VOTE SYSTEM; CONSTITUENCY;
D'HONDT METHOD; DROOP QUOTA; ELECTION;
ELECTORAL QUOTA; HARE SYSTEM; LIST SYSTEM;
PROPORTIONAL REPRESENTATION; SECOND BALLOT
SYSTEM; SINGLE TRANSFERABLE VOTE SYSTEM

Elite

The minority within a social collectivity (e.g. a society, a state, a religious institution, a political party) which exercises a preponderant influence within that collectivity. An elite which exercises preponderant *political* influence is called the ruling elite, or, by some writers, the political elite.

Elites may assume many different forms, but for ruling elites a major factor is the degree of elite-consciousness or organisation which they possess. Thus ruling elites, whether single (deriving from a common subgroup of society e.g. a social class, the military, a monolithic party) or plural (deriving from several such subgroups), may be a caste, a 'ruling class', an aristocracy of some form, or be lacking in any conscious linkages other than occupation of authority positions, such as the so-called 'establishment' in British society. It would appear that in complex, industrialised societies a degree of plurality of ruling elites is inevitable. This holds true even for societies which appear totalitarian in form.

Many elite theorists (e.g. Pareto, Mosca) have given attention to the concept of 'the circulation of elites'. This refers to the processes by which a ruling elite loses its power and is replaced by some new elite which has been acquiring power. This can be brought about, for example, by the existing elite having to recruit the more able members of other elites, either to perform political functions or to act as representatives of potentially competitive groups and thus to maintain the political support required by a ruling elite. These recruits are then able to act as a nucleus for a new elite. This substitution may also come about through revolution or similar violent change.

New members of elites are recruited by various processes, depending on the culture of the society and the nature and requirements of the ruling elite. Thus birth, educational attainment, professional ability, the acquisition of wealth, and the control of strategic political resources have all been major recruiting qualifications.

There have been many empirical studies of elites, but for many reasons the most thoroughly explored area of elite activity has been American local communities, by such scholars as Floyd Hunter, Dahl and Warner. A general survey of elites in politics is G. Parry, *Political Elites*, Allen & Unwin, 1969.

☞ ARISTOCRACY; CASTE; COMMUNITY STUDIES; OLIGARCHY; PLURALISM

Embargo

A law or regulation forbidding trade with specified countries, in general or with regard to specified items. It can thus be a political weapon, e.g. in time of war, or—in the case of a country or region in which war may be likely to occur—an embargo on armaments to that area may be a means of preventing war.

Emergency laws

Laws which come into effect on the formal declaration (by the head of state or the legislature, for instance) that a state of emergency exists, and which usually contain provisions for the exercise of legislative powers for the period of the emergency by some special body or by the head of state; they often include a statement of the procedure for terminating emergency powers, or a time limit beyond which such laws are no longer valid without renewal.

In some political systems, emergency laws are not explicit; the necessary powers are regarded as implicit in the constitutional provisions for government, rather than the matter for statute law.

Empire

An area, or group of areas, ruled by one authority (the emperor), and consisting of an imperial state and several other 'states', colonies or other dependencies. These dependencies will have been acquired generally by some means other than the voluntary acceptance of imperial rule by the submissive dependency; settlement, conquest and cession will have been the usual methods of acquisition.

Usually empires have consisted of a multiplicity of racial groups, with diverse languages, cultures and political systems. Thus the imperial powers have relied upon notions of an imperial religion, linguistic dominance, an imposed legal code, settlement by members of the imperial nation, etc., to unify and integrate their domains.

Examples of empires: the Roman empire; the Napoleonic French empire; the Austro-Hungarian empire; the British empire. Some authorities maintain that Russia, China and even the USA today may be considered to possess empires.

☛ COLONY; IMPERIALISM

Empiricism

The belief that experienced phenomena, rather than theories or ideas, are the basis of knowledge, and that, at best, only those hypotheses, theories and scientific laws which are validated by observable experience should be included in the body of accepted knowledge within a discipline.

Environment

The external stimuli to which a system is, or may be, responsive, are termed the environment of the system. Thus, for a political system, its environment consists of three categories of stimuli: those from other political systems; those from other subsystems of the societal system of which the political system is part, as well as from other societal systems; those from the physical environment. The political system may be involved in exchanges across its boundaries with any of these aspects of its environment, and each may impose stress on the political system.

'Environment' is also a concept employed in behavioural explanations of politics, where it refers to the external stimuli of an individual to which he may be responsive, and which may shape his political attitudes and behaviour. Here the distinction between actual and perceived environment is important, for the differences between them may explain aspects of the political behaviour of the individual.

☛ ADAPTATION; BEHAVIOURAL APPROACH; BOUNDARY; POLITICAL BEHAVIOUR; POLITICAL SYSTEM; STRESS; SYSTEMS ANALYSIS

Equilibrium

The state of balance or stability of elements of a system. The term as used in systems approaches to political analysis refers to the state of a political system when its elements are behaving in relation to one another in such a way that internal change will not occur. As this is an 'ideal type' case, systems will never reach a state of equilibrium, since novel conditions will continually occur to alter the behaviour of certain elements, which in turn affect the state of the system. However, the notion that systems may tend to approach a state of equilibrium may have a heuristic value for analytic purposes, though it implies a tendency to overlook the ideas of adaptation and development in a system.

☛ ADAPTATION; POLITICAL SYSTEM; SYSTEMS ANALYSIS

Escalation

The process whereby the actions of one actor in a situation (usually involving conflict, or the possibility of conflict) result in the reactions of another actor being at a higher level, as measured by e.g. the amount of force employed, the level of resources committed, or the type of response made. An arms race is one type of escalation; the progress of a war from conventional to nuclear would be another.

Escalation can also be applied to changes in the scope of a conflict, e.g. a limited war between two neighbouring states building up to the involvement of several states on account of a system of alliances or threats to national interests. The outbreak of the first world war was an example of such escalation.

☞ CONFLICT APPROACH

Ethnocentrism

The tendency to assess aspects of other cultures in terms of one's own culture, and thus in social science research to apply in a biased and improper fashion the standards and values of one's own culture in the study and analysis of other cultures. Such bias is often caused by an implicit or explicit belief in the superiority of one's own culture.

Ethnocentrism is particularly relevant as a problem in the fields of comparative politics and international studies.

☞ COMPARATIVE ANALYSIS

Executive

The branch of government responsible for the implementation of policies and rules made by the legislature. It thus includes as its members the leader of the government (e.g. prime minister, president, first secretary) and his colleagues, the political bureaucracy, whether permanent or politically appointed, and the enforcement agencies such as the police and armed forces.

In order to implement the policies of the legislature, executives in various states and other political organisations are frequently given the powers necessary to make implementing legislation (generally called 'delegated legislation'). The executive may also possess certain quasi-judicial powers, exercised through the operations of administrative tribunals.

In some contexts, the executive function or the executive as a branch of government may be referred to as the administrative function, or the administration.

☛ ADMINISTRATION; ADMINISTRATIVE TRIBUNAL; BUREAUCRACY; DELEGATED LEGISLATION; GOVERNMENT (A): the institution; SEPARATION OF POWERS

Exhaustive ballot

A method of voting in which successive ballots are taken, the candidate with the fewest votes being eliminated on each ballot, until one candidate secures an absolute majority.

☛ BALLOT; SECOND BALLOT SYSTEM

Experiment

A method of research by which a process is first defined, then observed under controlled conditions (and repeated as required), and the results noted. It is used to test hypotheses which have been previously asserted.

Experiments in political science are rare, being difficult to design in strict terms, due to the problems of defining all the relevant elements of the process to be observed, of isolating and controlling relevant factors, and of replicating the condition of the experiment. Small group studies and simulation techniques are methods of using experimentation on a limited scale.

☛ METHODOLOGY

F

Fabianism

As a general term, it refers to any strategy of gradualism and the avoidance of decisive confrontations (after the policies of the Roman general, Fabius Maximus). Fabianism in its more particular usage refers to the general philosophy of the adherents of the Fabian Society in Britain (founded 1884), which considers the proper strategy for socialism to be the use of existing political institutions, and the introduction of socialist reforms as a gradual process, rather than the more revolutionary tactics of other socialists.

Fabianism became extremely influential in the British Labour Party, on account of the reputation of its founders such as the Webbs, the growth of its membership, the realism of its policies and the importance of its research and discussion activities.

☛ SOCIALISM

Faction

A section of some larger organised group, often a political party, which has broken away to e.g. pursue a separate set of policies on some issue or range of issues, promote one of its members as leader of the whole group, follow strategies separate from those of the whole group, etc.

A faction may be organised less formally than the main group (e.g. the splinter group of a political party); it may possess a different style of leadership; it will, however, retain certain ties with the original group such as electoral campaigning on a united basis, common subscription to a basic ideology, or opposition to some other group.

Examples of factions: the Liberal-Unionists who followed Joseph Chamberlain in the late nineteenth century; the Bevanites and the Powellites in postwar British politics; the revisionist faction in the Spanish Falange Party; various groupings within the Indian Congress Party.

In the eighteenth and nineteenth centuries, 'faction' was also a term used, in criticism, as an equivalent to 'opposition', especially in the sense of opposing the public good or the national interest (e.g. as used in the *Federalist Papers* and British parliamentary rhetoric of the period).

☛ POLITICAL PARTY

Factor analysis

A mathematical method of analysing a relatively large number of variables, expressed in quantified form, in order to identify, and then to order in terms of the degrees of relationship which they are found to possess, a smaller number of regularities (the factors) which, it is proposed, those variables share. The calculations involved are statistical in form, as are the tests of the measure of relationship. Two essential preconditions, therefore, for the use of factor analysis, are precision in the concepts to be analysed and the availability of quantifiable data.

The correlations between the factors and the variables are expressed in the form 'variable A is related to factor x_1 to the degree 0·4, to factor x_2 to the degree 0·7 . . . etc.'. Factor analysis can be used in political analysis for the examination, for instance, of voting patterns and party affiliations or voting patterns and 'liberal' or 'conservative' attitudes of legislators, or to order the economic variables associated with international political power, etc.

☛ COMPUTER UTILISATION; MATHEMATICAL
   ANALYSIS; ROLL-CALL ANALYSIS; VARIABLES

Fascism

A political ideology, derived principally from the Italian movement (the *Fascisti*) which was led by Benito Mussolini and which took power in 1922. It directly influenced political movements in Germany (especially the Nazi Party), Spain, France, Britain and many other European countries, and movements which have had similar principles can be found in most industrialised states since the Second World War.

Its main principles generally must be inferred from the policies and activities of the movements, since they were rarely given coherent expression in the speeches or publications of the leaders or party publicists. They seemed to include militant anti-Communism (and, since they were regarded as ideologies akin to Communism, hostility to socialism, liberalism and democracy); the glorification of a leader, with dependence on his 'will' as the legitimate source of law, emphasis on a disciplined form of state organisation, in which secondary groups were obedient to the state, and this, though not necessarily implying a totalitarian form of state, would tend to impel it in that direction; the legality of only a single party, which was regarded as having a special protective and exemplary role in society; a strongly nationalistic programme, eschewing internationalism (among other reasons, because it was regarded as having connection with international Communism); the glorification of the nation (with the Nazi Party, of the race also), involving the destruction of the bourgeois culture of the immediate past and its replacement by a more distant, and myth-laden, culture (e.g. of the Roman Republic, or the Germanic legends); expansion of the boundaries of the state, by violence if necessary, in the name of self-protection or economic betterment; and economic control by the regime through some form of corporatism or organisational hierarchy responsible to the state, and in which conflict between labour and management, or between firms, was eliminated. It was also generally a basically 'irrational' ideology—and here its contrast to Marxism is particularly marked—with its emphasis on 'unreason' rather than 'reason' in politics, its glorification of the past, its accentuation of emotion and feeling as social forces, etc. Despite this contrast, many observers have remarked on the essential similarity of political methods used by Fascist and Communist regimes for attaining, exercising and preserving power.

Though seen by some interpreters as a class phenomenon (especially by the Marxists), Fascism in fact appears to have been hostile to all classes as such, seeing them as disruptive of the unity for which the state should strive. Other interpreters have viewed it as a historical phenomenon, being explicable only in terms of the particular economic and social conditions of the interwar years, and not applicable as a label to every type of racist or anti-Communist movement of the twentieth century.

Fascism can be regarded as a modernising force in many of the states where it has been influential, in so far as it has deeply opposed entrenched traditional interests and procedures, offered a strong sense of national identity, and emphasised the need for efficient social organisation.

☛ MOVEMENT; MYTH; TOTALITARIANISM

Federation

A state which consists of several regional governments and a central government, and in which both regional and central governments have powers over specified matters. These powers are almost invariably embodied in a written constitution, which states the matters with which regional governments are to be concerned, and the matters which are the concern of the central government, as well as specifying methods of resolving conflict between the two (often by some process of judicial review). Generally both governmental levels will possess taxing and enforcing powers, and both (in a democratic federation) will be elected directly by the people.

A federation differs from a confederation in that its citizenry are usually linked by ties of nationality while those of a confederation are of varied nationalities, and in so far as the federal union is regarded as indissoluble, in the main, whereas the nature of a confederate union is more fragile. A confederation will usually permit a much more limited range of powers to the central organs of government than is the case with a federation.

Examples of federal states include the USA; Switzerland; the German Federal Republic; Canada; Australia; Malaysia; India.

☛ CONFEDERATION; JUDICIAL REVIEW; UNITARY
STATE

Feedback

A concept, developed in the systems and communications approaches to political analysis, to indicate the process of conveying information about the state of the political system, or some specific part of it, or its environment, to structures within the system in such a way that the future action of those structures is modified in consequence. The results of such modification are then in turn 'fed back' to produce further modifications as necessary, and so on.

A feedback channel is any medium through which information may pass regarding the state of part of a system, to another part which is capable of modifying the behaviour of the first part. Feedback channels to and from the adjusting section of the system combine to form feedback loops, which may be regarded as circuits of information channels consisting of those through which information is conveyed regarding the state of part of the system to which they belong, and those through which responsive information is conveyed to adjust the state of that same part.

☛ COMMUNICATIONS APPROACH; SYSTEMS ANALYSIS

Feedback channel

☞ FEEDBACK

Feedback loop

☞ FEEDBACK

Feudalism

A system of social organisation, found mainly in Western Europe between about A.D. 900 and 1500, and characterised by a barter economy based on agricultural production, a complicated set of rather rigid mutual rights and obligations among a hierarchy of classes concerning matters of land tenure and military service, monarchical rule, and the existence of a landed aristocracy possessing wide discretionary powers of government within their domains.

The development of a more complex economic system based on money and urban commerce changed feudal societies into primitive capitalist societies.

☛ CAPITALISM; INDUSTRIAL SOCIETY

Field theory

A method of analysing the behaviour of individuals in social relationships, based primarily on the concept of the 'field' or 'life

space' of the individual as constituting the context of this behaviour. This life space is composed of the individual himself, his
psychological environment, and their interrelationships and
changes over time. It is particularly associated with the work of
Kurt Lewin (see his *Field Theory in the Social Sciences*, Tavistock,
1952), who proposed that the approach could be applied to the
behaviour of groups, as well as of individuals. As a scheme for
ordering data about social behaviour, it is of relevance to the
understanding of political behaviour, particularly regarding
perception of the environment, attitudes, the effects of social
change on individuals and groups, decision-making in groups, and
relations between groups and individuals.

☛ POLITICAL PSYCHOLOGY

Function

A function is a change, or the prevention of a change, in the state
of a system, or of some component in the system, as the consequence of the activity or existence of a structure. The function
may be such that no observable change occurs, but would have
occurred if the function had not operated (e.g. a stabilising or
feedback function). Functions may be potentially destructive of
the system (i.e. they may be considered 'dysfunctional') or may
aid its persistence or adaptation (i.e. be considered 'eufunctional').
Another distinction which can be made is between 'manifest'
functions (those that are recognised and intended by members of
the system), and 'latent' functions (those that would not so be
recognised or would be regarded as unintended by members of
the system).

☛ STRUCTURAL-FUNCTIONAL ANALYSIS; STRUCTURE

Functional representation

☞ REPRESENTATION

'Funnel of causality'

A conceptual framework used for accounting for a particular
decision at some fixed point in time, in terms of causal variables
which commenced their effect on the decision at various times in
the past. It was developed by A. Campbell and his co-authors in

The American Voter, Wiley, 1960, to account for voting decisions. In voting, for instance, a particular voting decision at an election can be seen to have been affected by a multiplicity of causal factors from the environment, or from the psychological make-up of the voter himself, at various times in the past, e.g. specific events of the election campaign, more distant events concerning initial party identification and support, adolescent and childhood influences, etc.

Using this framework, a variety of political, economic and social influences, of a wide range of specificity and diffuseness, can be identified as contributing to a particular decision, over a lengthy time-span. The relative importance of each of these influences is a matter for empirical determination. The framework can be used for ordering these influences, drawing attention to their mutual effect (by reinforcing, conflicting) and emphasising the time dimension. The problems of using the 'funnel of causality' are mainly concerned with the identification of *all* the relevant influences on a decision, and methods of measuring them.

☛ ATTITUDES; DECISION-MAKING ANALYSIS; PSEPHOLOGY

G

Game theory

Game theory is a formal mathematical method used to study decision-making in situations of conflict or bargaining, in which it is assumed that each player will seek his maximum advantage under conditions of rationality. Players may be individuals, or collectivities such as a committee. The framework of game theory consists of the players, a statement of their values, in quantified form, the rules and the 'pay-offs' for each combination of 'moves'. The result of any game may be determined (i.e. some one solution is logical as an outcome, given conditions of complete rationality), or indeterminate (i.e. no single logical outcome is obvious, as in the game of matching pennies).

Game theory usually concentrates on two-player games, as calculations and statements of strategies rapidly increase in complexity with games of more than two players.

The values which players attach to possible outcomes of the game must be quantified, in order to allow the calculation of optimal strategies and the pay-offs of the various outcomes. A strategy is a set of contingency instructions concerning moves in the game, designed to cope with all possible moves, or combinations of moves, of the opponent. The rules of the game state all the relevant conditions under which the game is played, such as which player moves first or whether moves are simultaneous; how moves are communicated; what information is available to each player concerning his opponent's values and strategies; whether 'threats' can be made binding; whether and to what extent side-payments are permitted; etc.

Games may be zero-sum (where the pay-offs to the players add to zero: what one loses, the other wins), or non-zero-sum (where certain outcomes are possible which give both players advantages or disadvantages, compared to other outcomes). The type of game known as Prisoners' Dilemma is a non-zero-sum game. Where the sum of the pay-offs varies according to strategies selected, the term 'non-constant-sum game' is applied.

An example of a simple zero-sum game (where pay-offs are stated as gains or losses to A):

		A	
		I	II
B	I	+3	−2
	II	+1	0

Suppose that A and B are candidates in an election. The television authority proposes a joint televised debate in the middle of the campaign. Each candidate has two strategies: to accept (I), or to refuse(II). If both accept, A will gain an extra 3 per cent of the vote (it is reliably estimated). This is strategy AI, BI. If A accepts and B refuses, A will win an extra 1 per cent of the vote (AI, BII). If both refuse, neither will gain or lose (AII, BII). If B accepts and A refuses, B will gain an extra 2 per cent of the vote (AII, BI). The logical outcome is AI, BII, as B knows A will accept and A knows B will refuse.

Problems of reducing real-life situations to the form of a game include the quantification of preferences; the finite nature of a game compared to the ongoing nature of political processes; the complications introduced by third parties or coalitions; the impossibility of achieving complete rationality in political situations; problems of communication between political actors; and the general distinction between the complications of actual situations and the formal rigour of game theory.

Nevertheless, game theory is a useful analytical technique, and has been employed in the study of international relations and strategy, campaign tactics in an election, coalition formation, legislative bargaining (logrolling), etc.

☞ BARGAINING THEORY; COALITION; CONFLICT APPROACH; DECISION-MAKING ANALYSIS; MATHEMATICAL ANALYSIS; PRISONERS' DILEMMA; SIDE PAYMENTS

Gaming

A type of simulation of an institution, process, pattern of events, etc., in which individuals assume roles relevant to the subject being simulated and play out those roles according to a more or less rigorous set of rules. The situation (or scenario) and the rules may vary widely.

While particularly applicable to situations simulating some aspect of international politics or military strategy, gaming may also be applied to competitive domestic political situations, e.g. an election; a committee hearing; legislative decision-making; budgeting, etc. It can be used as a device for learning about outcomes, or for research into the behaviour of the players, or both.

The term should be distinguished from 'game theory'.

☞ GAME THEORY; SCENARIO; SIMULATION

Gatekeepers

☞ SYSTEMS ANALYSIS

General theory

An explanatory system which claims to be able to account for all the relevant relationships among the elements of the subject or area with which it is concerned. In political theory, the explanatory systems associated with Marx, Bentley, Parsons and Easton are among the most general of the theories which have been developed, whereas those associated with Duverger (on political parties), Weber (on bureaucracy) and Deutsch (on political communication) are at a more particular level.

☞ THEORY

Generalisation

A statement which is, or purports to be, true of two or more items concerning some common factor, or set of factors, which they share.

A low-order generalisation is one that is true of a small class of items or in respect of relatively few common factors of a large class of items (e.g. the statement that all states represented in the United Nations Organisation possess armed military forces). Hypotheses tend, in political science, to be forms of low-order generalisation. A high-order generalisation is one that is true of a large proportion of factors of some class of item, and might amount to an explanatory theory.

☛ CLASSIFICATION; HYPOTHESIS; THEORY

Geopolitics

The study of the effects of the geographic environment—particularly in its physical, ethnic, demographic and economic aspects—upon the policies of governments. It is especially concerned with effects upon the foreign policies of states, and the conflicts that result from these.

The word is also used to indicate the ideology that emphasises the deterministic effects of such geographical aspects of the environment on the political development of states and racial groups. Such an ideology was influential, for instance, within the National Socialist Party in Germany between the two world wars.

☛ DETERMINISM; POLITICAL GEOGRAPHY

Gerrymandering

To apportion, or reapportion, electoral districts in such a way that the party responsible for making the apportionment gains an inequitable number of seats in the legislature. This is done, for instance, by concentrating the voters likely to vote for the opposition within the boundaries of a single constituency, where they will be in an overwhelming majority, while permitting neighbouring constituencies to be won more narrowly by the governing party as a result of such concentration. It thus depends on a nonproportional electoral system being in use. The term originates from a redistricting bill in Massachusetts in 1812, which gave undue advantage to the party of the Governor, Elbridge Gerry, and in which the boundaries of one of the new districts resembled a salamander.

☞ APPORTIONMENT; CONSTITUENCY

Goal attainment

One of the 'requisite functions' of social (including political) systems, as identified by Talcott Parsons. It is that function performed by those structures which are concerned with the selection and achievement of the aims (goals, policies) of the system, as well as with the methods of deciding among competing aims.

☞ ACTION THEORY; STRUCTURAL-FUNCTIONAL ANALYSIS

Government (A): the institution

The group of men, who, in their roles as members of certain institutions, make and implement policies in the form of binding decisions for a political community. The word also refers to the activity, or process, of making such authoritative policies.

While usually used to refer to the bodies which control states, the term can be applied to the authoritative policy-making institutions of any community, e.g. a city, a tribe, or an international organisation.

The general subdivision of government functions is into legislation (the making of authoritative policy); execution or administration (the implementation of policy); adjudication (the authoritative interpretation and validation of policy).

☞ ADMINISTRATION; ANARCHY; AUTHORITY; EXECUTIVE; GOVERNMENT (B): study area; JUDICIARY; LEGISLATURE; POLICY; REGIME; SEPARATION OF POWERS

Government (B): study area

The study of government is often regarded as equivalent to the study of politics, and is often found as an earlier word for 'political science'. More precise usage limits the word to refer to those aspects of political science concerned with the personnel, activities and institutions of 'governments', and usually of state governments at that. Whereas 'political science' may, by liberal interpretation, legitimately be applied as a term to refer to the study of political parties, elections, the politics of communities and small groups, as well as the politics of international organisations, 'government' as a study is usually restricted to the subjects of legislation, administration and adjudication as functions of the state.

The word is also used to distinguish the study of political events and structures from the study of political ideas, either historically or as political philosophy.

☞ GOVERNMENT (A): the institution; POLITICAL SCIENCE; POLITICS

Governor

Any person who is charged with the responsibility for governing a particular territory or people. More particularly, it is used to designate the chief executive officer in each of the states of the USA, and in Britain is the title of the Sovereign's representative in a colony.

Grounded theory

Theory which is generated by data obtained through the processes of social research, as contrasted with theory generated by deductive thinking from *a priori* statements, or ungrounded assumptions. Such theories, if they are properly constructed, are firmly linked to the underlying data and thus are difficult to refute. They are built up on the basis of categories and hypotheses generated by the data itself as recorded by the researcher. It is particularly associated as an idea with the work of B. Glaser and A. Strauss, especially as described in their book *The Discovery of Grounded Theory*, Weidenfeld & Nicolson, 1968.

☞ THEORY

Group basis of politics

An approach to political analysis based on the premise that the group, rather than the individual or the state, is the basic unit of political activity, since individuals in politics act in group contexts and their behaviour is affected—some would even say determined —by group structures, norms, goals, etc.

The first major statement of the idea was that of A. F. Bentley in *The Process of Government*, Chicago University Press, 1908. Since the Second World War several political scientists have taken the idea further, including E. Latham, in *The Group Basis of Politics*, Cornell University Press, 1952, and David Truman, whose book *The Governmental Process*, New York, Knopf, 1951, explores many of the secondary concepts involved in the group approach, such as access, group tactics, etc.

A 'group' is defined as a 'mass of activity' (Bentley), or a relatively persistent pattern of human activity and interaction. Accidental collectivities such as crowds, or analytic collectivities such as married men or new voters are not groups within the terms of these definitions. Individuals, of course, may be members of many groups simultaneously, but this does not affect the view of group theorists that any individual's political activity can only be given meaning in the context of some group to which he belongs.

Such a theoretical approach has consequences for the explanation of political activity at the societal level. 'Interests' are defined as the 'activity directions' or 'policy attitudes' of groups; unrepresented interests may exist, but their identification will imply the potential existence of groups to press for these interests, as the need for certain policy outputs from the authorities become greater. The state, or other political authority, is seen as a 'cash register' whose outputs (in the form of decisions or policies) represent the balance of group pressures at any one time.

Among the subjects for further analysis, group theorists would include styles and functions of group leadership; the membership and interaction characteristics of groups; the strategies of group activity, including relations with other groups; societal norms that affect group activity, such as the 'climate of opinion' about interests and groups themselves; the determinants of the effectiveness of group activity in any specified situation. A case study which links many of these problems into an explicit theoretical framework is H. Eckstein, *Pressure Group Politics*, Allen & Unwin, 1960.

Major criticisms of the approach focus on the difficulty of defining the concept of 'group' satisfactorily, without making it so general as to be meaningless, the tendency to ignore the autonomous role of state institutions, and the difficulty the approach seems to have in satisfactorily accounting for individual political

H

Hare system

A method of voting based on the single transferable vote system, by which the voter ranks his preferences among the candidates (1, 2, 3, 4, . . . etc.). The seats are then allocated by means of the calculation of the electoral quota, which in this case is the result of dividing the total number of valid votes cast by one more than the number of seats to be filled; then follows the redistribution of the surplus votes of those candidates who have more than the necessary quota of first preferences (and who are therefore elected), then the redistribution of second and subsequent choices of those with the least number of first preferences, and so on until a sufficient number of candidates achieve the quota to fill all the seats available. Though originally developed on the basis of a single national constituency, in practice multi-member constituencies of about 3–7 members are used.

☛ ELECTORAL QUOTA; SINGLE TRANSFERABLE VOTE

Head of state

The occupant of that political office which is responsible for acting as leading representative of the power and authority of the state, as indicated by such functions as the formal declaration of war or a state of emergency, the accreditation of ambassadors and their reception from other states, the appointment of the prime minister (or the equivalent officer) and his governmental colleagues, the award of honours and assent to legislation. These functions vary from state to state, but are basically similar in most states.

The head of state may be appointed by right of birth (e.g. the British monarch), chosen by some group (e.g. a general following a military coup), elected, directly or indirectly (e.g. French Presidents in the Fourth and Fifth Republics, the President of the USA), or be imposed by external force. The term of office may be fixed and limited, or be for life. The extent to which the powers of the head of state are limited by law and custom also varies considerably from state to state, and from time to time (e.g. the declining powers of the British monarch, the expanding powers of the American President).

☛ ABDICATION; LEADERSHIP; MONARCHY; SOVEREIGNTY

Hegemony

The predominance of one unit within a group of such units; thus, in politics, the dominant position of one province in a federation (e.g. of Prussia in the Second Reich), or of one state in a confederation (e.g. of France in the European Economic Community), or of one person in a committee or other body (e.g. of Napoleon in the Consulate period of the French Revolution).

Hierarchy

The ranking of persons or political offices on the basis of the authority or political power each one possesses. Thus there is a hierarchy within the British Cabinet, within the Central Committee of the Russian Communist Party, within the party organisation of the American Senate, etc. Informal hierarchies exist as well as formal ones, e.g. in the political system of a community, within international organisations such as the UNO, etc.

The term is also applied to those occupying the most powerful positions within an organisation, in a collective sense, e.g. the Roman Catholic hierarchy, which includes the Pope, the Curia, the College of Cardinals, etc.

☛ STATUS

Hypothesis

A hypothesis is a proposition or assertion concerning a conjectured relationship between two or more elements of some area under study or investigation, made in a form such that empirical consequences can be deduced, and then tested. On the result of these tests, the hypothesis is tentatively accepted, or refuted. A hypothesis is usually stated in the form of an affirmative proposition, or a question.

☞ LAW (A): scientific law; METHODOLOGY; THEORY; VALIDATION; VERIFICATION

I

Ideal types

The concept of 'ideal types' is associated particularly with the work of Max Weber, e.g. in his analysis of forms of leadership, though many examples exist in the social sciences, ranging from the *Republic* of Plato, through the constructs of classical economics (e.g. perfect competition), to contemporary political analysis (e.g. 'perfect rationality' in decision-making and policy analysis).

The concept is valuable because an ideal type emphasises an extreme, unattainable and limiting case of some sort, within some more extensive classificatory scheme. Actual examples may thus be compared with the ideal type case, and the differences noted. Since ideal types tend themselves to be complex constructs, this facilitates the comparison and classification of complex social phenomena.

☞ PARADIGM; TYPOLOGY

Ideology

Ideology is a concept used to designate the primary values which people possess, and which enable them to impose some kind of mental order on the diverse individual and social experiences which they meet. A political ideology is thus the set of primary values from which a person derives his attitudes towards political events and problems, and which guide his political conduct.

Authorities differ as to the degree of explicitness, integration and internal consistency which any set of primary values should possess in order to be termed an ideology, but it may be most useful to employ the term in its widest sense, to refer to any related values which are not derived from prior values. This in turn gives rise to the notion of a 'ladder of values' by which in logical, though not necessarily actual, progression social decisions derive from policies, policies from programmes and programmes from ideologies. Thus a decision to nationalise a particular steel company may be the result of a policy of steel nationalisation, which is part of a programme which includes nationalisation of basic industries, which is ultimately derived from an ideology of socialism. An ideology of free enterprise leads to a legislated programme of monopoly regulation, a policy of prohibition of certain types of merger, and a particular decision to forbid a proposed link between two firms.

It is more difficult to restrict the use of the term 'ideology' only to those value sets which are explicit and internally consistent, for, while several ideologies have been made explicit (e.g. Marxism, Catholicism, anti-Semitism), they are rarely, if ever, completely internally consistent. In any case, for each individual they depend upon personal interpretation and application, which itself increases the chances of inconsistencies arising.

In the context of a society, an ideology may be congruent with, or opposed to, the prevailing values of that society. However, it cannot remain unaffected by experience within that society, and ideologies become modified (though not necessarily rationally) to take account of such experiences. An example is the modification of Marxism that occurred in the decades between the Bolshevik Revolution and the Second World War.

☛ 'LADDER OF VALUES'; VALUE SYSTEM

Image

A mental picture of some person, group or object formed as a result of past perceptions, and modified by experiences. It is often evaluative in form. Images may be important in affecting attitudes and opinions, but also they may be influenced by such attitudes and opinions. The 'party image', for instance, which a person holds, may be regarded as a factor in influencing whether he votes for that party at an election.

Sometimes the word is used in a collective context, to refer to the mental picture held by a group, e.g. 'the image of the President held by college students'.

☛ ATTITUDE; OPINION; STEREOTYPE

Impeachment

Accusation before a competent tribunal of a public official for crimes of e.g. impropriety, misdemeanour or corruption in the exercise of his office. In Britain, where the House of Lords tries such cases on the accusation of the House of Commons, the last recorded case was in 1806. In the United States it is provided for under both federal and state law. At the federal level, the House prepares articles of impeachment, and the Senate acts as the tribunal. The case of President Johnson (1868) is the most famous.

It is rarely used as a remedy nowadays, being replaced by actions in the civil courts, or the application of political remedies such as the resignation of the accused from his office.

Imperialism

The belief system that one country could, and should, expand its rule over other political communities and territorial areas, not necessarily contiguous or ethnically similar, for purposes of economic self-advantage, military security, international prestige, and the furtherance of some ideology or 'civilising' mission. Such an expansion of rule, when it has occurred, is termed an 'empire'.

Imperialism differs from colonialism in that colonialism is systematic only in its economic aspect of dependency on trade to the benefit of the colonising power, whereas imperialism is the systematic creation of a multipurpose dependency relationship with several different areas or territories. Colonialism frequently involves a policy of settlement; imperialism need not. Colonial status is always a status of inferiority; in an empire some states may possess considerable degrees of internal autonomy and a political status of near-equality with the imperial power (e.g. the status of Canada in the nineteenth-century British empire, or of Bavaria in the German Second Reich).

An important feature of imperialism appears to be the attempted imposition of administrative, legal and even cultural and religious unity on the dominions of the empire. The Roman and British empires are clear examples, and their successes in this aim are indicated by the importance accorded by historians to the 'civilising' effects of Roman imperial rule in Europe, and by the transformation of the British empire into a quasi-voluntary Commonwealth, with its persistent cultural and economic links.

Less precise usage, following in many cases the Marxist employment of the word, which applies 'imperialism' as a descriptive term to a particular type of capitalist economic development, employs the term to mean any type of rule by one state over another, e.g. to American intervention in Asia and Latin America, or to Russian interference in the internal affairs of Hungary, East Germany and Czechoslovakia.

☛ COLONIALISM; COMMONWEALTH; EMPIRE

Index numbers

A system of measuring changes in the state of some variable, by which its state as measured at an initial point in time is given as 100, and subsequent changes are then expressed as percentage increases or decreases on this base (e.g. an increase of 40 per cent from the base date would be expressed as 140). A set of measurements can be taken for periods before the base date, as well as after. Index numbers can be used for comparing changes in two or more variables over a period by basing them on their state at the base date, and expressing changes as relative percentages, e.g. in population size and national income, or unemployment rates in two different occupations.

Indirect election

☞ ELECTION

Industrial society

A type of society in which the style and shape of social, political, economic and legal institutions are affected by the existence within that society of an economic order based largely on industrial production. In such a society, agriculture represents only a small sector of the economy, at least in terms of employment. Urbanisation has resulted from the need to concentrate large numbers of workers near factories and other places of employment. Social structure reflects the influence of industrial production, e.g. on classes, family structure, occupational divisions.

In terms of politics, an industrial society will probably exhibit many of the features of mass society; it may or may not be democratic, but almost certainly political leaders will have to take account of the existence of large, concentrated masses of population in urban areas, and of the needs of trade unions and industrialists when policy is under consideration. The media for political as well as other types of communication will be of a cheap and concentrated form, e.g. the press, broadcasting, outdoor display publicity.

The diversity of industrial society will give rise to numerous political interests, which may be represented by political parties, lobbies, interest groups, or (in one-party totalitarian states, for example) by informal groupings. While such organisations contribute to the politicisation of the population, the process may be uneven, and problems of anomie and alienation may arise.

The general process of change from a pre-industrial society to an industrial society is associated with changes, which are often termed the process of political development or modernisation, in which traditional and undifferentiated institutions in politics give way to 'modern' and highly differentiated political institutions. A discussion of this process with reference to Germany is the basis of R. Dahrendorf, *Society and Democracy in Germany*, Weidenfeld & Nicolson, 1968. In Britain such changes took place in the late eighteenth and the nineteenth centuries; in the USA mainly in the period between the Civil War and the New Deal. Russia is still undergoing such changes, while India and China have hardly started on the process.

☛ ALIENATION; ANOMIE; MASS SOCIETY;
  MODERNISATION

Influence

Influence is a factor which, other things being equal, may alter the behaviour of an individual in a desired direction when the influence is exercised. While some writers do not differentiate between influence and power, there would appear to be advantages in the distinction drawn by others, that influence is a concept denoting uncertainty regarding the likelihood of desired effects being produced when A exercises influence over B, compared to the much higher degree of probability of production of desired effects when A exercises power over B. Influence tends to be exercised in a competitive context (e.g. the influence of a pressure group on the Government when an item of legislation is pending); power is more usually monopolistic in any one context (e.g. the power of the prime minister over his Cabinet colleagues, or the power of the President over the armed forces of the USA in wartime).

☞ POWER

Initiative

A formal proposal by citizens, or the electorate, to be accepted as legislation or as a change in the constitution by the legislature. It is thus a form of intermittent direct democracy. Several constitutions of states of the USA, and cantons of Switzerland, allow for legislative or constitutional initiative, either in an advisory form (i.e. allowing the legislature to vote on it in the normal way) or in a mandatory form (i.e. requiring the submission of the proposal to the whole electorate). The requisite number of signatures supporting an initiative proposal may be based on a fraction of the electorate, or may be a fixed minimum number.

☞ DIRECT DEMOCRACY; RECALL (A): the institution

Input-output analysis

A method of describing, classifying and explaining political phenomena in terms of the structures and processes of the political system which are involved in converting various inputs into outputs.

Both Easton and Almond have developed frameworks for input-output analysis. Easton's systems approach summarises the inputs from the environment of the political system, or from the system itself, as demands and support; the outputs, following complicated filtering, aggregation and conversion processes, are authoritative decisions and actions. Feedback processes take place which link the input and output stages. Almond has related input-output analysis to structural-functional analysis, by classifying his inputs and outputs as functions. They include the inputs of political socialisation and recruitment, interest articulation and aggregation, and political communication; and the outputs of rule-making, rule application and rule adjudication.

An important advantage of the input-output approaches to

political analysis is that they can be applied to the analysis of any type of political system, and are not confined in application to states, certainly not to states of the modern, industrialised variety, possessed of competitive party systems. They also permit the analysis of system change, by their use of the concepts of feedback and communication.

☛ POLITICAL SYSTEM; STRUCTURAL-FUNCTIONAL ANALYSIS; SYSTEMS ANALYSIS

Inputs
☞ INPUT-OUTPUT ANALYSIS

Institution

A network of structures, procedures and shared values within a social system, of a relatively permanent nature, which is concerned with some social function or group of functions. Examples of institutions concerned with political functions are: the Supreme Court of the USA (the function of conflict resolution concerned with interpretation of the Constitution); the United Kingdom Parliament (the functions of rule-making, and control of the executive authorities, among other things); the electoral systems of democratic regimes (the function of political recruitment and selection for authority positions).

Insurrection

Armed resistance against governmental authority and its executive agents, for purposes of e.g. resisting the imposition of legal constraints, overthrowing the government or weakening its authority.

☛ COUP D'ÉTAT; PUTSCH; REBELLION; REVOLUTION

Integration
☞ POLITICAL INTEGRATION

Intelligentsia

The members of a society who are generally highly educated, who pursue occupations in which the communication of abstract ideas is a paramount factor (e.g. teaching, artistic production and criticism, types of journalism, scientific research), and who may be regarded as possessing certain attitudes towards political issues in common, particularly where these affect the cultural aspects of their society.

In some contexts, the term is used widely, to refer to the educated classes generally, especially the urban educated classes in developing societies. In other contexts it is limited in application to the groups of people who devote much of their time to speculative thought and its propagation, particularly on political matters.

Interest

An interest forms the basis of a demand for action by the political system, made by an individual as a result of his attitudes, personal characteristics, economic requirements, etc. If an interest is consciously shared by several individuals, they may make joint demands on the system as an interest group. Such interests may be religious or ideological (e.g. a demand for Sabbath observance), ethical (a demand for the abolition of capital punishment), economic (a claim for a protective tariff), social (a demand for a lowering of the age of majority), etc. The direct beneficiary need not be the person making the demand.

Interests are aggregated in order to be more influential in their claim for attention by the political authorities. The agents of aggregation may be interest groups (e.g. trade unions, employers' federations, civil rights organisations), pressure groups (e.g. the groups formed in Britain to retain, and to abolish, capital punishment, the American groups opposing the American military presence in Vietnam) or political parties. Through interest aggregation, demands become issues for political consideration and action, e.g. by being incorporated into governmental policy programmes.

☛ GROUP BASIS OF POLITICS; INTEREST ARTICULATION; LOBBY; PRESSURE GROUP

Interest aggregation

☛ AGGREGATION; INTEREST

Interest articulation

The processes whereby opinions, attitudes, beliefs, preferences, etc., are converted into coherent demands on the political system.

These processes include the activities of a variety of structures and institutions, e.g. the programmes of political parties, the efforts of interest groups, electoral campaigns, and a multiplicity of channels, e.g. the mass media, direct action, petitioning, interpenetrating elites. A failure of interest articulation processes may lead to stress, and consequent political disruption.

Interest articulation is one of the functional requisites identified particularly with the analytic work of Gabriel Almond, e.g. in G. Almond and G. Powell, *Comparative Politics: a developmental approach*, Little, Brown, 1966, and G. Almond and J. Coleman, eds., *The Politics of the Developing Areas*, Princeton University Press, 1960.

☛ INTEREST; STRUCTURAL-FUNCTIONAL ANALYSIS

Interest group

☛ INTEREST; PRESSURE GROUP

International politics

The political aspects of relationships between states, and the international institutions and processes through which such political relationships are conducted. Such relationships may be cooperative, competitive, or conflicting.

Various approaches have developed in the field of international politics. Among the more generally employed have been the power approach (associated particularly with Morgenthau and Schwarzenberger); conflict approaches; systems analysis (e.g. in K. Holsti, *International Politics: a framework for analysis*, Prentice-Hall, 1967); institutional approaches (e.g. several studies of the United Nations Organisation); policy analysis; communications approaches; and the application of formal models such as game theory. Gaming, simulation and case study methods have also been used as aids to study and for testing hypotheses concerning international politics. A concise survey of several of these approaches is given in C. McClelland, *Theory and the International System*, New York, Macmillan Company, 1966.

Problem areas on which scholars have concentrated include the making of foreign policy and the institutions through which it is made operational (formal diplomatic channels, propaganda media, international agencies, etc.); the relationships between diplomatic and military-strategic policies; the functioning of the international political system, and of the various subsystems contained within it (e.g. alliances such as NATO, areas or regions such as Latin America, Eastern Europe); war, including its avoidance, political prosecution and terminal settlement; relationships of power and influence between states (e.g. in a bipolar or multipolar power distribution); the organisation of international political institutions; movements towards supranational political communities (e.g. the EEC); trends towards world government.

☛ ALLIANCE; BIPOLARITY; BLOC; CASE STUDY METHOD; COMMUNICATIONS APPROACH; CONFLICT APPROACH; GAME THEORY; GAMING; INTERNATIONAL RELATIONS; MULTIPOLARITY; SIMULATION; SYSTEMS ANALYSIS

International relations

The relationships between states (and their peoples), which concern the policies they adopt toward each other with regard to their national interests, the methods of contact and communication (including warfare, economic sanctions, etc.), the operation of international institutions, the formation of alliances, coalitions and blocs, the development of international law, and the identification of the economic, social and political customs and conventional practices that exist.

It is an interdisciplinary field of study, involving particularly history, sociology, economics, law and political science, and, more recently, social psychology (see, for example, H. Kelman, ed., *International Behaviour*, Holt, Rinehart & Winston, 1965).

The study of international politics is a major part of the study of international relations.

☛ INTERNATIONAL POLITICS

Interpellation

A device used in some legislatures for the purposes of obtaining information from a minister by means of a formal, written question regarding some aspect of policy or administration for which that minister is responsible. Generally it must be made known to the minister several days in advance, and there may be other requirements such as a minimum number of supporting signatures of members of the legislature. The rules of the legislature will also state whether, and under what conditions, debate or a vote may occur following a reply to an interpellation.

The device was employed in the French Fourth Republic, and is still used in the Italian and Swiss legislatures.

☞ RESPONSIBILITY

Interview

A conversation between two persons by means of which the interviewer hopes to obtain information relevant to some study or research upon which he, or his employer, is engaged.

An interview may be structured, i.e. may consist of a previously determined pattern of questions and comments by means of which the interviewer tries to obtain relevant responses, possibly within a restricted range (e.g. 'yes-no' answers, or answers related to quantities); or unstructured, i.e. the broad purposes of the interview are kept in mind, but the pattern of questions and answers is deliberately kept flexible. Interviews may be part of a sample survey, or may be used for other types of survey (e.g. biographical studies of all the members of some group); the content may be factual, straightforward and easy to cross-check with other sources, or may consist of responses that reflect subconscious information, by means of depth interviews, for instance.

Though usually conducted on a face-to-face basis, interviews may be carried out by telephone or other long-distance media of communication.

☞ DEPTH INTERVIEW; SURVEY

Investiture

The formal procedures associated with the induction of a person into some high office, usually of a political nature, involving ceremonial, the bestowal of insignia, etc. The investiture of the Prince of Wales is an example.

Iron law of oligarchy

The proposition, put forward by Michels in his study of the organisation of political parties, that organisations inevitably develop in such a way that there is specialisation of leadership roles, and that the occupants of these roles are not only desirous of maintaining their positions as leaders, but are in fact enabled to do so by their ability to manipulate and control important aspects of the organisational structure (e.g. rules, resources, communication, procedures, the timing of meetings).

☞ OLIGARCHY

Irredentism

The ideological basis of some movement or party which seeks to incorporate within its state some territory of which the state has been deprived in the past, or some ethnic group believed to be similar to that constituting the population of the state.

The term originated with the late-nineteenth-century Italian political party called the Irredentist Party, who sought to recover areas of claimed Italian territory still under non-Italian rule, including the South Tyrol, Trieste, Corsica and Malta. Other examples of irredentist policies: the Indian policy towards Goa before its reincorporation within the Indian state, and Spanish policy toward Gibraltar.

Issues

Matters concerning which there are two or more incompatible sets of attitudes, and which thus give rise to conflict. Such conflict may be resolved by political procedures (i.e. through procedures laid down in advance, and subject to some recognised authority), or by war, social processes, legal adjudication, etc. Thus issues which have been dealt with by political means include the abolition of capital punishment for murder in Britain; the introduction of emergency powers in West Germany; the limitation of incumbency of Presidents in the USA; the dispatch of a military force to the Congo by the United Nations. Issues decided by non-political means include the prevention of the creation of a Biafran state by the Ibos; the return to orthodox Communist policies in Czechoslovakia; the ending of the doctrine of 'separate but equal' segregated education in the USA.

The term is also employed in systems analysis to refer to matters capable of decisional outputs by the political authorities; wants and demands become converted to issues.

☞ CONVERSION PROCESS; SYSTEMS ANALYSIS

J

....

Judicial legislation

Rules, declarations or judgments made by members of the judiciary, which have the effect of adding to, or changing, the content
of the law. This may be the result of previous ambiguities inherent in a statute, which are then resolved through litigation.
Major decisions of the USA Supreme Court are often examples of
judicial legislation.

☛ JUDICIAL REVIEW; JUDICIARY; LAW (B): stipulative
law

Judicial review

The process whereby a court or tribunal consisting of members of
the judiciary decides on the constitutionality of laws, rules or
actions of the legislative or executive branches of government.

It is thus one method of settling disputes concerning the
interpretation of written or unwritten constitutions, but is not
found in all states. In the United Kingdom the doctrine of parliamentary supremacy prevents such disputes from arising; in one-
party states the settlement of disputes is secured by party fiat; in
theocracies the priesthood regard themselves as the sole interpreters of the law and hence of its constitutionality. Judicial
review is found in many federal states, where it is used to adjudic-

ate on constitutional disputes regarding the division of central and local powers. It is thus important in the United States of America (where the Supreme Court assumed the power of judicial review in the important judgment of *Marbury v Madison*, 1803), in the German Federal Republic (where the Basic Law provides for a Constitutional Court to review the constitutionality of legislation, as well as e.g. the constitutional nature of political parties, under Article 93 of the Basic Law), Australia, India, etc.

☛ CONSTITUTION; FEDERATION; JUDICIAL LEGISLATION

Judiciary

The judiciary is the branch of government responsible for interpreting authoritatively the laws made by the legislature and administered by the executive branch, in cases where disputes arise as to the meaning, validity, or supposed breach of such laws. In most politically developed states, the judiciary consists of professionally trained judges, appointed or, in some cases, elected, though some judicial systems provide also for the presence of lay assessors on the bench. The selection of judges, their relations to the political process, the effects of their decisions on the law, and the factors which influence judicial decision-making, have all been topics of interest to political scientists.

☛ ADMINISTRATIVE LAW; ADMINISTRATIVE
TRIBUNAL; EXECUTIVE; JUDICIAL LEGISLATION;
JUDICIAL REVIEW; LAW (B): stipulative law;
LEGISLATURE; SEPARATION OF POWERS

L

'Ladder of values'

A term applied to the notion that personal values vary in specificity, and that logically, if not historically, it is possible to trace a specific expression of opinion to some more abstract or more comprehensive value expression, such as an attitude, and that in turn these can be related to a more fundamental ideology. The term does not imply that there is always logical consistency, either horizontally among all opinions, attitudes or elements of an ideology, or vertically between an opinion and an attitude, etc.; it only points to relationships.

The term can also be applied in the context of groups, e.g. political parties, to indicate the derivation of policies from programmes, and programmes from general manifestos, party constitutions or other general statements of party values.

☛ ATTITUDES; IDEOLOGY; OPINION; VALUE SYSTEM

Latent function

☞ FUNCTION; STRUCTURAL-FUNCTIONAL ANALYSIS

Law (A): scientific law

Statements regarding the relationship between two or more elements, and which have been found to hold true in a sufficiently large enough number of cases, may be termed scientific laws. A group of such laws, combined in such a way as to provide wider explanations of certain types of phenomena, may be termed a theory.

Scientific laws may be absolute (in the form 'condition X always is associated with effect Y') or probabilistic (in the form 'there is a probability of Z per cent that condition X will be found to be associated with effect Y').

☛ HYPOTHESIS; LAW (B): stipulative law; THEORY

Law (B): stipulative law

The term 'law' refers to the rules made by a legislative agency within a political system, by processes or procedures recognised as legitimate, which direct human conduct within that system. They are binding on the whole community (or some stated part of it, e.g. martial law) and are supported by coercive sanctions such as imprisonment, damages, or loss of property, as imposed by the judicial authorities. The legislative agency is not necessarily, in every political system, a structurally distinct institution. In tribal communities or small organised groups, for instance, it may consist of the total membership of the society.

Argument often arises over the definition of 'law' with regard to those laws which are not regarded as legitimate in terms of their content. It would appear, however, that much of the essence of the term 'law' is concerned with the acceptance of the legitimacy of the procedures for making the law, rather than its content.

☛ AUTHORITY; COERCION; JUDICIARY; LAW (A): scientific law; LEGITIMACY; REGULATION (B): rule; RULE

Leadership

Leadership is a pattern of behaviour which has as its purpose the organisation and direction of the efforts of a group towards desired ends. Political leadership is found where the desired ends are political. It is situational behaviour, in that leadership (as distinguished from authority or influence) is dependent on specific contexts of a leader, followers, goals, and methods of goal attainment. The acceptance of leadership by followers depends on their regard for the legitimacy of the leader, as well as e.g. on his likely efficacy, and this legitimacy may depend upon his occupancy of a formal authority role.

On the other hand, Max Weber's classificatory scheme of 'ideal types' of leadership underlines the varieties of bases for leadership-acceptance. He distinguished charismatic leadership (when leaders are obeyed because they are thought to possess extraordinary or magical attributes), traditional leadership (when leaders are obeyed because they occupy some status in society which has previously been entitled to obedience, e.g. by birth into a ruling dynasty or class) and 'legal' leadership (based on authority arising out of a rationally established set of rules and procedures).

As well as the basis of leadership authority, leadership styles also vary. Some leaders are persuasive, others forceful, yet others conciliatory. Efficacy appears to depend less on the possession of any one style, than on the ability to choose and adapt styles in the context of task, means available and attributes of followers. The differences between Churchill and Attlee in Britain, Stalin and Trotsky in the USSR, Franklin Roosevelt and Truman in the USA, Nehru, Shastri and Mrs Gandhi in India, illustrate the variety of leadership styles – and levels of success – available in modern states.

Recruitment of political leaders is provided for in different ways in different political cultures. Patterns of education, differences of social class, types of leadership position available, limitations imposed on certain wouldbe recruits (e.g. women, members of certain ethnic or religious groups, people under a certain age) all influence the availability of leaders. But it is necessary to note that both formal and informal processes affect leadership recruitment, and also that the demands of a crisis may permit the rise of leaders who might otherwise never have been considered, e.g. Hitler, de Gaulle, Winston Churchill.

☛ AUTHORITY; 'BOSSISM'; CHARISMA; DEMAGOGUE; DICTATORSHIP; ELITE; HEAD OF STATE; LEGITIMACY

Legislature

The institution of government which has the power of making, amending and repealing laws for a society. It may be elected, appointed or hereditary in composition, or some mixture of these. It may consist of several chambers, or of just one; in most states a bicameral form of legislature is preferred.

Though, paying regard to the principle of the separation of powers, many states have different principal institutions for legislation and administration, politically it is difficult to maintain an absolute distinction of function, and delegated legislative powers are often given to executive bodies.

☞ ADMINISTRATION; BICAMERAL; DELEGATED
LEGISLATION; SEPARATION OF POWERS

Legitimacy

The principle which indicates the acceptance on the part of the public of the occupancy of a political office by a particular person, or the exercise of power by a person or group, either generally or in some specific instance, on the grounds that such occupancy or exercise of power is in accordance with some generally accepted principles and procedures of conferment of authority.

The exact nature of such principles and procedures varies from society to society, and over time, but many of them include certain symbolic rituals which serve the function of solemnising conferment, pinpointing it in time, and ensuring that the attention of the public is given to it. Such legitimate conferment may be held, for example, to stem from a supernatural source (as in the election of a new pope by the College of Cardinals, or the leadership of the Mahdi in the Sudan in 1881), from hereditary descent (as in the proclamation of accession, and later the coronation, of a British monarch), from the electorate (as in the inauguration ceremonies of the President of the USA), or from higher governmental authority (the appointment of a senator to fill an unexpired term in the US Senate, or the appointment of a British prime minister, for instance).

While legitimacy is difficult to measure of itself, certain empirical indicators can be employed, depending on their degree of reliability. Among these might be the level of coercion in a society required to implement policies, the number and capabilities of attempts within a state to overthrow the government, or the leader of the government, and the occurrence of civil disobedience, rebellion, civil war or similar disruptions.

☞ ALLEGIANCE; AUTHORITY; LEADERSHIP; POWER

Liberalism

A set of beliefs based on the assumption that there should be as much individual freedom as possible within any civil society, allowing for the existence of essential constraints, and that the individual, not the state, society or any other collectivity, is of supreme importance in social life.

It developed mainly in the eighteenth and nineteenth centuries, and can be seen as a philosophic reaction to the forms of arbitrary rule that existed in the western hemisphere in that period. It was associated with various movements concerned with political, religious, economic and social emancipation e.g. the nonconformist denominations in England, anti-slavery, some of the groups pressing for independence in the American colonies, utilitarianism and the philosophic studies of John Stuart Mill, and reform movements in several countries concerned with women's rights, 'trust busting', the penal system, education, the electoral system and universal suffrage, etc. In Britain, the Liberal Party, developing out of an alliance between the Whigs and radicals, attempted to put liberal ideas into practice under such leaders as Gladstone, Asquith and Lloyd George. In America, liberalism found room in both major parties for some of its programmes. In Germany and France there was a tendency for liberal political parties to be small, disunited and ineffectual in a party system dominated by major groups to the left and the right.

Liberalism, like many broad-range ideologies, is difficult to define in terms of specific content, but probably the following principles would be acceptable to most liberals is so far as they accept also the basic assumptions of individual liberty stated above: the 'rule of law' on an impersonal and impartial basis; the creation and amendment of laws on principles of rationality; the limitation of state power to the minimum necessary for the preservation of civil order, the safety of the state and the achievement of the social conditions necessary for a liberal society; the free choice of governments through fair and universal elections; an economy based on free choice and free exchange (though some liberals would claim that government intervention in various forms – e.g. monopoly legislation – is a precondition of a free market), and the unhindered international exchange of goods; the explicit statement, and the protection, of civil rights; the abolition of unwarranted social, political and economic privilege; a pluralistic social order based on the free creation and operation of groups.

Liberalism does not necessarily imply egalitarianism, though it may, in order to achieve its aims of freedom in society, stress 'equality of opportunity'. Nor is it necessarily nationalistic, except in so far as national independence from imposed external rule is a precondition of individual liberty and a social order in which such liberty can flourish. Indeed, despite the historical association of liberalism and nationalism in Europe, today liberals are among the strongest advocates of suprastate forms of political organisation: a federal Europe, based on the political development of the Common Market, the United Nations, and the cause of world government.

A succinct analysis of liberalism as a philosophy is found in K. Minogue, *The Liberal Mind*, Methuen, 1963.

► CONSERVATISM; IDEOLOGY; PLURALISM;
    RADICALISM; SOCIALISM; UTILITARIANISM

List system

A system of election, based on proportional representation of parties or similar groups, each of which presents a list of candidates. The voter then casts his vote for one of these lists. In some systems the voter can alter the content, the order, or both, of the list itself. Various methods of calculation of seats per list are used, such as the d'Hondt method in West Germany, or some system of quota and greatest remainder. The list system is also employed in voting for the Italian Chamber of Deputies, the Knesset of Israel, the Swiss National Council, and the legislature of Finland, among others.

► D'HONDT METHOD; ELECTORAL SYSTEM;
    PROPORTIONAL REPRESENTATION

Lobby

The term has several associated meanings, depending on context. As a verb, to 'lobby' is to attempt to exercise influence on legislators, in an attempt to persuade or coerce them into taking some decision favourable to those lobbying. In the context of British parliamentary practice, 'the Lobby' refers to the area within the confines of Parliament, but not in the legislative chambers, where Members of Parliament and peers may meet with those journalists to whom the privileged status of 'lobby correspondent' has been granted (and who are also referred to collectively as 'the lobby').

Despite a tendency among some authorities to prefer a wider use of the term to act as a synonym for pressure groups or interest groups (e.g. see S. Finer, *Anonymous Empire: a study of the lobby in Great Britain*, Pall Mall Press, 1958, especially chapter 1 : What is the Lobby?), a more restrictive definition is preferred by others. Such a definition would distinguish 'lobby' from pressure group and interest group by using it to refer to groups specifically organised for the purposes of influencing legislators, though such groups may be composed of other groups which would qualify for the title of pressure group or interest group. Thus H. H. Wilson's study, *Pressure Group: the Campaign for Commercial Television*, Secker & Warburg, 1961, deals with the groups which comprised the pro- and anti-commercial television lobbies in the controversy over the introduction of commercial television in Britain in the 1950s. Other examples of British lobbies are the Arab lobby and the road transport lobby; in the USA the oil lobby and the war veterans lobby are well known; West Germany has a refugee lobby and a road haulage lobby, among others.

A lobbyist or lobby agent is a person who directly represents the views of a lobby to the legislators; in the USA, for instance, many salaried lobbyists are registered under the Federal Regulation of Lobbying Act (1946). In Britain there is no such provision for regulation, though professional lobbyists exist.

☛ INTEREST; PRESSURE GROUP

Local government

Local government is the process by which certain public functions and services are carried on within a given set of territorial units in a state. The extent of these functions and services differs from state to state, and over time, but will generally consist of the exercise of certain discretionary powers given to local authorities by the state (e.g. by means of legislation such as the Local Government Act, 1958, or the London Government Act, 1963), and the administration of certain services on behalf of the state, though it must be noted that other such services may be administered more directly by local branches of state agencies.

An important variable in local government is the organisational structure of local authorities. In England and Wales, for example, there are single-tier authorities (the county boroughs), two-tier authorities (Greater London; the non-county boroughs and urban districts within counties), and three-tier authorities (parishes within rural districts within counties). Changes in this complex structure are expected as a result of the findings of the Maud Commission on Local Government, which were published in 1969.

Local government systems, in which the local units possess no powers independent of the central government, should be distinguished from federal systems, in which the federal units do possess such independent powers (though local government exists in federations also).

☞ DECENTRALISATION; DEVOLUTION; FEDERATION; LOCAL GOVERNMENT STUDIES

Local government studies

The section of political science which is concerned with the development, structure, functions and organisation, personnel, and policies of local government, and with its relationship to other political and social organisations, especially those of central government.

Many of the methods of analysis employed in other fields of the discipline may be used for studying local government, and interdisciplinary study is also frequent, e.g. studies of local government organisation in combination with specialists in public administration, the study of elites in local government with sociologists, problems of local government planning with economists, environmental planners and lawyers.

Research in this field has influenced many aspects of local government reform, with regard to structure and organisation as well as to policies and functions. It has also been important in devising forms of local government for newly independent states.

Among the more specific areas of study of local government politics have been: voting and participation; leadership in local government organisations; parties and interest groups in local politics; relations with central government departments and agencies; local government policy formation.

☞ COMMUNITY STUDIES; LOCAL GOVERNMENT; REGIONAL STUDIES (A): domestic regions; URBAN STUDIES

Longitudinal studies

Studies of individual elements over successive periods of time, e.g. in panel studies of electors' preferences and attitudes, in order to analyse changes in the attitudes and behaviour of those elements. Such studies may take the form of questionnaire-based surveys, panel studies, observations, etc., and are in contrast to studies concerned with static analysis of a situation at some given point of time, e.g. case studies, or surveys of opinion based on a single interview questionnaire.

☛ CROSS-SECTIONAL ANALYSIS

M

'Machine politics'

Political situations where the influence of a highly organised party structure, controlled – possibly corruptly, perhaps with the aid of violence – by a 'boss', is exercised over patronage appointments, electoral campaigns, selection of candidates, and the policy process where this affects local affairs. The party machine operates in the political interests of its leadership, rather than those of its membership, the public, or the national party organisation.

'Machine politics' is associated particularly with urban politics in America, but is sometimes applied to local politics in other states where control is in the hands of a small, self-perpetuating elite of a local party.

☛ 'BOSSISM'

Macro-politics

That part of political science which is concerned with the description and analysis of political aggregates such as the state, confederations, international politics, political parties, etc. A major organising concept in macro-political studies is the *political system*, interacting with its environment.

☛ MICRO-POLITICS; POLITICAL SCIENCE; POLITICAL SYSTEM

Majority

The section of a group constituting more than one-half. In politics, for example, the number of votes constituting a majority is equal to 50 per cent plus one of votes cast (sometimes referred to as an 'absolute majority'), though some procedures require a majority to be 50 per cent plus one of possible eligible votes, i.e. to take account of abstentions.

Special majorities are those requiring some higher proportion than 50 per cent plus one; two-thirds or three-quarters are common examples (e.g. as in the amendment process of the US constitution). The United Nations Security Council and the Council of Ministers of the European Economic Community are institutions which require certain forms of special or qualified majorities on particular types of question.

Secondary usages are: to indicate the difference in votes between e.g. two candidates in an election, or those favouring and against a particular proposal; and to refer to the group, coalition, or party constituting more than half of a legislature, committee or similar body.

The word is often misused to mean a plurality.

☛ MINORITY; PLURALITY

Mandate

The commission regarding policy given by the electorate to a legislature or a legislator, or claimed by a government by virtue of its success in an election on the basis of a declared programme.

The existence of a mandate is difficult to establish through normal electoral procedures, except in the most general terms, since most governments and members of legislatures are elected under party labels and on the basis of multiple-policy programmes. It is more legitimate to use the term in a negative sense, to deny that a mandate exists to introduce some policy not foreshadowed in the electoral programme, and for which no emergency need exists.

A second use of the word 'mandate' is to refer to the decrees issued by the League of Nations to certain member states after the First World War, requiring them to administer certain territories on a temporary basis, and under specified conditions.

☛ REFERENDUM

Manifest function

☞ FUNCTION; STRUCTURAL-FUNCTIONAL ANALYSIS

Manifesto

A published statement of political beliefs and policies, originating from an individual or, more usually, a political movement or political party.

It may be intended as a fundamental guide to some movement or group concerning its aims, e.g. the Communist Manifesto published by Marx and Engels, or as a statement of intentions on the basis of which an electorate can decide which party it wishes to vote into office, e.g. the manifestoes of the British parties at general elections, or the 'platforms' of the American political parties in presidential elections.

Marxism

The system of thought regarding the interrelationships of history, economics, politics and social life based on the writings of Karl Marx (1818–83), particularly in the *Communist Manifesto* (1848) and *Das Kapital* (first volume published 1867). Marxism was one of the major influences on the development of socialism in nineteenth-century Europe, and, more particularly, on the growth of Communism. As interpreted and modified by Lenin, it became the official ideology of all the Communist regimes established from 1917 onwards, though this has not prevented major conflicts of interpretation, many of which have had serious political consequences, e.g. in Russia (the Trotsky–Stalin quarrels, for example), in China, and within the bloc of East European satellite states.

Marxism, though never stated as a doctrine in any coherent or systematic form by Marx himself, can be seen to include the following main ideas:

—that the norms, values, class structure, etc., of a society are those most appropriate to the prevailing mode of economic production;

—that differences between societies can be reduced to differences in their class structures, which in turn derive from their form of economic organisation, e.g. feudal, capitalist, socialist;

—thus social behaviour is explicable, and is only explicable, as class behaviour, and that since class interests are irreconcilable, social conflict consists of, and is caused by, class conflict;

—that the predominant system of production in industrialised societies at the time he wrote was capitalist, and that according to historical laws, it was doomed to destruction (as had been all previous systems) because it contained within it important 'contradictions', e.g. its associations with imperialism and war, the trade cycle, the increasingly miserable state of the proletariat, and the perpetuation of class conflict;

—that though reforms (e.g. as proposed by Social Democrats) may postpone revolution, none the less revolution was inevitable, and that after the revolution the 'dictatorship of the proletariat' will lead to Communism;

—in Communist society, class interests will disappear, and thus also class conflict, leading to the 'withering away' of the state as a coercive regulator of social relationships.

While serving as an ideology for the Communist movement, Marx's theories have also provided for social science several useful insights, especially regarding elites, social class and revolution. For political science more particularly, his theories have been valuable in emphasising the relationships between political and economic factors in society, even if many political scientists would not accept Marx's insistence on the dependence of politics on economics.

☞ BOLSHEVISM; CAPITALISM; COMMUNISM;
  INDUSTRIAL SOCIETY; REVOLUTION; SOCIALISM

Mass media

Those media of communication which are channelled toward an undifferentiated audience, by methods which preclude personal modification of the message by sender or receiver during transmission. Thus, in industrialised societies, the mass media include radio and television broadcasting, newspaper production, the cinema and poster advertising. As a result of aiming at a large and undifferentiated audience, the production of messages by use of the mass media is relatively inexpensive.

☞ MASS SOCIETY; POLITICAL COMMUNICATION;
  PROPAGANDA

Mass society

A society, usually highly urbanised, industrialised and heavily populated, in which the major institutions, processes and communication patterns are organised to deal with the population as a basically undifferentiated aggregate. Power is centralised, and local or regional autonomy discouraged.

Because of the division of labour inherent in large-scale industrialisation and the nationally organised market for products and skills, the population tends to be very mobile, and thus has few opportunities for developing social relationships of more than a transitory character outside of the family. Political participation through voluntary organisation is low, partly because the opportunities of political influence available to the individual appear to be few, partly because of the difficulty of developing voluntary political organisation in a mobile society. The media are organised for, and their communication content is based upon, a national and undifferentiated audience.

While mass society is possible under political conditions of 'mass democracy', where the government is responsive to large-scale interests such as industry, the professions and unions, and the military, mass society is invariably found under totalitarian rule also.

An analysis of mass society in its political aspects is to be found in W. Kornhauser, *The Politics of Mass Society*, Routledge & Kegan Paul, 1960.

☛ ALIENATION; ANOMIE; INDUSTRIAL SOCIETY; MASS MEDIA; TOTALITARIANISM

Mathematical analysis

The increased interest (especially during the second half of the twentieth century) taken by political scientists in quantification and model-building involved closer relationships between political analysis and mathematics.

Mathematical analysis allows the use of a formal language which is, of itself, value-free; it aids in the formulation of hypotheses and laws in a more precise manner than might be obtainable by other means; it permits the exact measurement of effects, changes of state, processes, etc.; it can be used to demonstrate implications by application of its own logic that might be unperceived if in non-mathematical form.

The range of uses of mathematical analysis is wide. Not only does it allow for more precise description, conceptualisation and operational definition, it permits a better appreciation of relationships between variables, it allows the construction of complicated theories in quantitative form, and the testing of them. Among the types of analysis which may be used in political explanation are: game theory; causal path analysis; factor analysis; various types of statistical theory; graphical methods; measures of variance, etc.

Several fields of political science have found applications of mathematical techniques of value for analytic purposes. In election studies, the cube law is an interesting example of a mathematically based, partly validated hypothesis. In various types of political research, including attitude and opinion research, surveys based on sampling and probability techniques have been important. Content analysis has been used in domestic and international situations, and based on mathematical manipulation of quantities, for the generation of hypotheses and their testing. In international politics game theory, attitude measurements, variance tests, and many other types of mathematical analysis have been used. (For a sampling, see J. Singer, ed., *Quantitative International Politics*, New York, Free Press, 1968.) Legislative redistricting, the effects of electoral systems on party and other types of representation, dimensions and correlations of politics (see e.g. A. Banks and R. Textor, *A Cross-Polity Survey*, Massachusetts Institute of Technology Press, 1963), economic approaches to political choice, and small group political behaviour are among other fields of research where mathematical techniques of analysis have been important.

It must be remembered, however, that despite the advantages of mathematical analysis, particularly as aided by computer utilisation, hypotheses, models and theories using quantitative elements will be no more reliable than the precision and the appropriateness of the quantities in relation to the qualitative elements under study. This problem, with others relating to the uses of mathematics in politics, is dealt with in H. Alker, *Mathematics and Politics*, New York, Macmillan Company, 1965.

☛ COMPUTER UTILISATION; CONTENT ANALYSIS; FACTOR ANALYSIS; GAME THEORY; STATISTICAL ANALYSIS

Metapolicy

Policy which deals with the organisational arrangements of policy-making, including the capabilities of policy-making personnel, the processes of obtaining and using information relative to policies under consideration, the integration of policy-making agencies and ways of improving the efficiency and 'rationality' of decisions. The term is employed particularly in the works of Y. Dror, and especially in his book *Public Policy-making Reexamined*, San Francisco, Chandler, 1968.

☛ POLICY; POLICY ANALYSIS; POLICY APPROACH

Methodology

The study of the utility and validity of methods of investigation, in the context of a particular scientific discipline or area under consideration. Also, the selection of such methods, in advance of an investigation, that are considered likely to be appropriate and fruitful.

Methodology in political analysis is thus concerned with the various models, classifications, and conceptual schemes that exist, the techniques that are available for investigatory purposes, research procedures used in the past, and their validity, etc., all for the purpose of discovering new knowledge and ordering it meaningfully, or in order to test existing propositions.

☛ POLITICAL ANALYSIS

Metropolis

The chief town or city of a region, province or state, though the term is often used to refer to any important town. A metropolis is not necessarily governed as a unit.

☛ CITY; CONURBATION; METROPOLITAN POLITICS

Metropolitan politics

The study of the political organisations and activities of large cities. Since the administrative responsibility for the government of a metropolis may be divided among several local authorities (e.g. London before the creation of the Greater London Council; metropolitan New York), such study cannot be confined to a study of e.g. city councils.

☛ CONURBATION; LOCAL GOVERNMENT STUDIES; URBAN STUDIES

Micro-politics

That part of political science which is concerned with the description and analysis of the political behaviour of individuals or small groups, rather than of political aggregates such as the state or a mass party. Micro-political analysis is usually focused on the relationships between the actor (a person or small group) and the environment of that actor, including the norms, rules, structures, etc., that the actor is involved with. Micro-political studies include aspects of political psychology, small-group analysis, conflict studies, etc.

☞ MACRO-POLITICS; POLITICAL BEHAVIOUR; POLITICAL PSYCHOLOGY; POLITICAL SCIENCE; SMALL GROUP POLITICS

Militarism

The attitude or practice which increases the role of the military in the state to one of dominance, in terms of policy-making, social control and the statement of social values.

Such domination may come about by means of a coup on the part of the military, by a revolution, as a result of the increasing pressure of external threats, through cultural development, etc. It will probably involve the formal occupation of political authority roles by members of the military, including those of head of state, head of the government, ministers, bureaucrats, communications controllers, etc.

Studies of militarism have centred around the comparative causes, forms and methods of military control of political power (e.g. S. Finer, *Man on Horseback*, Pall Mall, 1962); the styles of military leadership; militarism in developing countries (e.g. M. Janowitz, *The Military in the Political Development of New Nations*, Chicago University Press, 1964); and the ideologies of militaristic regimes.

Examples of militarist states have included Japan in the period from 1931 to the end of the Second World War; Germany under Prussian hegemony in the period from the Franco-Prussian war to the armistice in 1918; Greece following the coup in 1967; and several Latin American states where, following military coups, the armed forces provide the political authorities and set the political norms of the society.

☞ CIVIL-MILITARY RELATIONS

M 126

Minority

A group which is less than half the total membership of some larger aggregate of which it is part. In voting, the number of votes or voters constituting less than 50 per cent of the votes cast. In a society it refers to an ethnic, regional, religious or other group possessing distinctive identity and outnumbered heavily by the rest of the population.

☛ MAJORITY

Mobilisation

The process by which members of a political community are brought into situations which involve them in political affairs. One form of such involvement is voluntary participation in politics, by membership of parties, movements, interest groups, etc., by voting, by attendance at political events, involvement in political discussion and similar activities. But, especially in totalitarian, modernising or non-democratic 'mass' societies, mobilisation may well involve forms of coerced participation, such as demonstrations, attendance at rallies, voting where choice is absent and turnout compulsory, forced membership of political organisations (e.g. the professional party groups for teachers and lawyers under the Nazi government in Germany), etc.

☛ PARTICIPATION

Model

A model is an abstract system (which may be represented verbally, mathematically, physically, graphically, or in other ways), to represent some or all of the properties of an analogous system of relationships. Examples include a computer simulation of aspects of the economy, a set of equations representing key factors in the international arms race, a diagram representing patterns of communication flows within a political system. Models may be used for purposes of simplification, hypothesis-testing and the generation of further hypotheses.

☛ ANALOGIES; METHODOLOGY; SIMULATION

Modernisation

The term is often used as a close synonym for 'development', but is usually preferred on the grounds that it more readily draws attention to the total nature of social change, and that it avoids presuppositions of 'improvement' or teleological views of the modernisation process inherent in concepts of development.

Modernisation may be defined as the process of social change which involves economic advancement, specialisation of political roles, the pursuit of 'rationality' in policy formation, technological development, and fundamental alterations in social patterns (e.g. urbanisation, social and geographic mobility, the formation of secondary groupings, educational advancement), all of which enables a society based primarily on traditional values and institutions to assume the characteristics of developed, or modern, societies (i.e. societies with highly complex, specialised and industrialised economic systems, advanced technologies, bureaucratised political institutions, etc.).

The study of modernisation involves, in addition to a sensitive appreciation of relevant aspects of the cultures of modernising societies, an integrated knowledge of the concepts, theories and techniques of several of the social and behavioural sciences, and an awareness of the complex inter-relationships of social, economic, political, psychological and cultural factors involved in social change. An example of a study of interest to political scientists which demonstrates such integration is D. Apter, *The Politics of Modernisation*, Chicago University Press, 1965. Also of interest is the collection of essays, including several dealing with cross-disciplinary subjects, edited by Apter and entitled *Some Conceptual Approaches to the Study of Modernisation*, Prentice-Hall, 1968.

☛ DEVELOPMENT STUDIES; POLITICAL DEVELOPMENT;
TELEOLOGICAL EXPLANATION

Monarchy

The form of rule in which there is a single head of state, with the title of king (or queen) or its equivalent; in which the position of head of state usually descends by heredity; and where the monarch is believed to be possessed of religious or similar symbolic importance for the state and its institutions.

Associated more especially with feudal and medieval periods of history, few monarchies exist today in which the political, as well as symbolic, importance of the monarch is significant. The series of revolutions from the American War of Independence and the French Revolution onwards have replaced monarchies by republican oligarchies, democracies or totalitarian dictatorships. The United Kingdom, the Scandinavian countries and Holland are examples of states where monarchy has persisted, though its revival in Spain appears probable, as a result of decisions by General Franco.

☛ DYNASTY; HEAD OF STATE

Monism

The belief that the state is, and should be, the supreme and ultimate source of the laws regulating a society. While monism does not exclude the existence of subordinate political or other social groups, it does deny that they possess any autonomous legal powers against the supremacy of the state.

☛ PLURALISM; SOVEREIGNTY

Motivation

The term used to indicate those causes of the behaviour of an individual which arise from his own personality. While the psychologist uses the term to focus on the psychophysiological drives that lead to certain types of behaviour given certain stimuli, and sometimes on the unconscious urges underlying conscious activity, in politics the term has acquired a wider meaning, to include attitudes, values, opinions, etc., regarding the situation or object towards which behaviour is directed. Thus support for a policy of restriction of immigration might be 'motivated' by unconscious fears or wishes related to the sex impulse or the desire to protect territory, by attitudes concerning immigrants, by opinions about the effects of this policy on the electoral popularity of one's political party, etc.

Motivations may thus be conscious or unconscious, and, like attitudes, have to be analysed primarily through their expression, particularly in verbal statements or goal-directed behaviour.

☛ ATTITUDES

Movement

A collective grouping that seeks to bring about major changes in social institutions, or (in the case of revolutionary movements, e.g. an independence or separatist movement) even an entirely new order, involving the use of political means at some stage.

Movements may attract relatively large mass support, or be confined to a small number of followers. They are distinguishable from pressure groups because of the fundamental nature of their aims, their lack of reliance on a single organisational base, and their disregard of subtle political tactics. They differ from political parties because they do not always seek to exercise the functions of government, and again because they lack a unified organisation; however, they may support candidates for office in elections. Yet they are more permanent than a mere crowd, and more purposeful than an unorganised 'interest'.

A major feature is their possession of some very basic common purpose, or even ideology, which in turn generates a strong sense of group identity, and may encourage the emergence of charismatic leadership. A movement may transcend existing divisions of social class, religion, party affiliation and even nationality. Examples are: the suffragette movement, the student movement, the working-class movement, the civil rights movement in the USA, the black power movement, and the European movement in Western Europe.

A movement may change into a political party, or may be captured by it (e.g. the Populist movement in the USA), or it may create its own party as a 'vanguard' organisation without losing its character as a movement. Alternatively, a movement may become organised as a pressure group, losing some of its ideological quality but gaining a sharper political profile and embracing a more deliberate and sophisticated set of political tactics.

☛ INTEREST; POLITICAL PARTY; PRESSURE GROUP

Multi-party system

☞ PARTY SYSTEM

Multiple election

☞ ELECTION

Multipolarity

The clustering of elements around several points on some scale. In political discourse, it is used to refer to the situation in international politics where several major powers, with lesser allies and client states, exist, rather than where two major powers or blocs exist (bipolarity). It may also be used as a term to refer to electoral situations where support is scattered among several competing parties, rather than divided for the most part between two major parties.

☞ BIPOLARITY; POLARISATION

Myth

A myth is an account of some past event or process in a community, which is in some way a distortion of reality, and often based on irrational or even supernatural foundations, but which embodies in symbolic form valued norms or beliefs of that community.

N

....

Nation

A group of people, often, but not invariably, occupying a single territorial area, who possess a common historical and cultural tradition which is strong enough to preserve a common political organisation for them if they already possess one, or to stimulate political or military activity to obtain such an organisation.

The force of the idea of 'nation' is often sufficient to persist in the face of occupation, partition, dispersion of the population, incorporation into a federal or imperial state, industrialisation and other fundamental changes. Examples of nations which have persisted in this way include the Jews, the Poles, the Germans and the Irish.

Definitions of the word also exist, based on subjective criteria, in which a nation is any group of people who believe they possess (whether they do or not) a common historical and cultural tradition. This is found e.g. in some African states, which depend on the creation of a sense of nationhood to preserve political integration.

☞ NATIONALISM; STATE

Nationalisation

The process of taking under the ownership and control of the state some commercial enterprise previously under private ownership and control. The enterprise is then normally operated either directly by a government department, or indirectly through the medium of a public corporation.

Nationalisation is associated with political ideologies of a socialist or collectivist type. It is usually directed first at the public utilities (gas, water and electricity supply, coal and steel production, transport undertakings) but may extend to any type of economic activity.

☛ COLLECTIVISM; COMMUNISM; SOCIALISM

Nationalism

An ideology based on the premise that states should be organised on the basis of nationality, and that, for any specific nationalist movement, some particular nation has not yet achieved statehood, or has not achieved it as completely as it should.

Historically, modern nationalism has its roots in the eighteenth and nineteenth centuries, and was especially influenced by the French Revolution, Napoleonic conquests and the nationalist revolutionary movements of the first half of the nineteenth century. The postwar settlements of 1918–19 with their emphasis on 'national self-determination' and the anti-colonialism of the period following the Second World War were also important in stimulating nationalist movements, especially in modernising areas of the world, such as Africa and the Middle East.

Nationalism can be allied to other doctrines and ideologies, e.g. Communism (as in North Vietnam), apartheid (as in South Africa and, to a lesser extent, Rhodesia), democracy (as in nineteenth-century France), militarism (as in Prussia), and religious beliefs (as in Pakistan).

While relying on such factors as a common language, a shared history, territorial contiguity, ethnic similarity and a shared culture, nationalism defies definition in terms of precise objectively identifiable components, depending more on a subjective belief in belonging to a common 'nation' than on objective tests of nationhood.

Works which examine aspects of the concept of nationalism include K. Minogue, *Nationalism*, Batsford, 1967, and K. Deutsch, *Nationalism and Social Communication*, Massachusetts Institute of Technology Press, 1953, which also contains a useful bibliography.

☛ NATION

Nepotism

The act of favouring members of one's own family, or one's close relatives, by offering them appointments to office, awarding them official contracts, or otherwise using one's political position to favour them improperly. The test of nepotism is whether or not it is likely that the favoured relative would have secured the appointment, contract, etc., if the familial ties had not existed.

While a form of patronage, it is only one particular subcategory of it.

☞ PATRONAGE

Neutralism

A policy with regard to the international status of a state, by which it determines and announces its intention of refusing to join military alliances. More particularly, states which pursue such policies today have in mind the military blocs associated with Russia and the USA, and their neutralism extends primarily to the systems of alliances which those blocs involve. Such policy may also be termed 'non-alignment'. India, Sweden and Indonesia are major examples of self-declared non-aligned states.

Such a policy may be pursued for reasons of military security; as a means of procuring development aid from both the Russian and western camps; as a moral posture, in the hope of acting as mediator or a channel of communication; etc. Attempts have been made to coordinate the foreign policies of non-aligned states, e.g. at the Bandung Conference, 1955, but with little success.

A comprehensive study of neutralism is contained in P. Lyon, *Neutralism*, Leicester University Press, 1963.

☞ NEUTRALITY

Neutrality

A legal condition in international relations, whereby a state declares its intention not to be a party to a conflict, either by hostile actions against one or other of the belligerents, or by extending privileges of trade, etc., to either belligerent without also extending them to the other. In return, the neutral state expects its territory to remain inviolate, and its trade and other activities to be unhampered, as far as possible, by the actions of the conflicting powers. Such neutrality can be declared in advance, either with regard to a potential conflict between stated parties, or generally with regard to any external conflict. Neutrality may be imposed on a state as a condition of a treaty, for example; this process is termed 'neutralisation'. An example of a neutralised state is Austria, following the Second World War and the four-power agreements regarding her future status, 1955.

☛ NEUTRALISM

Nominating convention

☞ CONVENTION (A): the institution

Norm

In social science, the word 'norm' refers to a shared group value which is used to judge the social behaviour of group members. Some norms are explicit, such as laws and regulations, and enforced by legitimate formal sanctions; others are implicit, and enforced by informal sanctions. The prohibition of the bribing of electors in most democratic countries takes the form of an explicit norm. Social pressures against coloured people have long been methods of enforcing implicit norms in the community, the work-place and other social institutions of Britain and the USA.

The term is also used in statistics, to refer to a measure of central tendency (such as an average, a median or a mode).

☛ NORMATIVE STATEMENT

Normative statement

A statement which expresses a value shared, or expected to be shared, by a social group. It may be in the form of a rule, a law, a command, or similar imperative, or in the form of a description or request.

☛ NORM; VALUE JUDGMENT

Normative theory

A systematic explanation of values or ideals, including the reasons why they are held, the effects they may have on behaviour, their interrelationship with other values, etc. A normative theory may also seek to provide grounds for the prescription of values, e.g. Marxist theory or democratic theory.

☛ NORM

O

Observation

The term refers to the focused attention of a person on some phenomenon, for the purpose of noting its behaviour, or some specific aspect of that behaviour.

It may also refer to the result of an act of observation, in some recorded form, e.g. 'Three successive observations of the sample of voters interviewed showed that there was no relationship between political opinions on specific issues and the number of hours spent viewing political television broadcasts during the campaign.'

☛ PARTICIPANT OBSERVATION

Oligarchy

A system of government based on rule by a small, unrepresentative and self-interested elite group. Because of its normative overtones, the term is generally avoided in political analysis in favour of some other classifications of concepts used in elite analysis.

☛ ARISTOCRACY; ELITE; IRON LAW OF OLIGARCHY

Ombudsman

Originally a Scandinavian office (where the term means 'Procurator'), the institution known as the Ombudsman has been adopted in several countries, though at times with a change of title. The United Kingdom and New Zealand each have a Parliamentary Commissioner, West Germany a Parliamentary Commissioner for Military Affairs, etc.

While the details concerning powers and areas of jurisdiction vary from state to state, the Ombudsman in general has the task of receiving complaints from citizens aggrieved by some alleged decision or action of public officials, and which decisions or actions perhaps cannot be appealed to the courts of law. Having agreed that there is a prima facie case of 'maladministration'— such as improper use of powers, irrelevant criteria being applied in the exercise of discretion, erroneous interpretation of the law— the Ombudsman may investigate the complaint and make a report to the legislature. In some countries, he may himself initiate prosecutions in the courts.

In some countries, some of the functions of the Ombudsman are carried out by a system of administrative courts, but these courts, unlike the Ombudsman, are not agencies of the legislature.

☛ ADMINISTRATIVE LAW

Operational research

A term originating from the use of statistical and other scientific techniques to analyse and resolve complex problems in the Second World War, operational research now means the application of quantitative techniques, usually on an interdisciplinary or multidisciplinary basis, to the decisional or functional problems of any organisation, including government.

☛ STATISTICAL ANALYSIS

Operationalisation

The process of converting definitions of concepts into 'operations' of measurement, which enables empirical tests (preferably of a quantitative nature) to be made for the presence, absence or extent of a phenomenon, and permits the combination of concepts to be made from which laws and theories can develop.

It is recognised that an operational definition may not be fully equivalent to the original meaning of the concept, and that operational definitions may only be possible for some part of a concept's meaning. But unless a concept is, at least in part, capable of operationalisation—even if only of the simplest kind—it will similarly not be capable of unambiguous communication to another observer.

Thus, of the many possible definitions of democracy, one which included such operational measures as the proportion of the adult population entitled to vote, the frequency of opportunity for changes of government, and the number of effective political parties seeking election as governing parties would be less ambiguous, and more precisely determinable, than one cast in terms of 'the will of the people' or 'government of the people, by the people'. The adequacy of the operational indicators would, of course, be a matter of argument but before, rather than after, they are made.

☞ DEFINITION

Opinion

An expression of judgment by a person concerning the attributes of an object, person or process about which there is, at least potentially, some dispute. Opinions derive, at least in logical terms, if not historically, from underlying attitudes, and indeed, one way of discovering and measuring these attitudes is through the collation of opinions. The techniques used for attitude scaling may also be applied to the measurement of opinions.

☞ ATTITUDES; ATTITUDE SCALING; 'LADDER OF VALUES'; OPINION LEADER; PUBLIC OPINION

Opinion leader

A person who is influential within a community or other social collectivity in forming the opinions of others, by virtue of his being regarded as an authoritative or reliable source of information, and whose own views are often taken as models by others. An opinion leader need not necessarily hold a position of formal authority, or control communications resources, though both may be relevant to establishing a reputation as an opinion leader.

The notion of opinion leaders is included in the two-step theory of communication flow, which postulates that most people obtain their information and form their opinions about social matters via intermediary agencies such as opinion leaders, rather than directly from the news services, etc.

☛ COMMUNICATIONS APPROACH; OPINION; POLITICAL COMMUNICATION

Opposition

A position of disagreement or antagonism; thus, in politics, disagreement with the policies or programme of a government. Also, by extension, the term is applied to a group, or collection of groups, who so oppose.

The rights and duties of opposition vary among different political communities. In some states, the function of opposition is formalised, as in the British Parliament, the American Congress, the West German *Bundestag*; this formal recognition may be given through extra remuneration and a defined political status for the leader of the opposition, the right of reply to public statements by the government, and the right to be consulted on certain bipartisan matters such as legislative schedules and procedure, declarations of war, and arrangements for state ceremonies. In other states (as in Britain before the mid-nineteenth century) opposition may be termed 'faction', and regarded as opposition to the state as well as to the government of the day, and so, especially in one-party states, as being near-treasonable.

☛ FACTION

Ordering

The establishment of a relationship among a set of items, which is both asymmetrical (i.e. the order relationship holds between A and B, but the same relationship does not hold between B and A), and transitive (i.e. an order relationship between A and B, B and C, is also an order relationship between A and C). An order relationship may be based on discrete quantitative properties (e.g. age, annual income, size of majority at the last general election), or on points on some continuum (e.g. strength of attitudes regarding some object). Typologies and classifications may be based on forms of ordering.

☛ CLASSIFICATION

Organisation

A social group, possessing identifiable boundaries and a common subculture, which has been deliberately formed for the purpose of pursuing some goal or objective by joint effort. A political organisation is therefore a group which has been created to pursue political objectives.

☛ GROUP BASIS OF POLITICS; ORGANISATION THEORY

Organisation theory

The framework of concepts by which the study of organisations, their characteristics, behaviour, membership, etc., is conducted.

Several of the research methods of the social sciences have been used to study organisations, including the creation of typologies (e.g. Weber's 'ideal types', Etzioni's classification of organisation types), participant observation, simulation, interview-based surveys, communication analysis, sociometric techniques, systems models, etc.

The main interests of organisation theorists have been the interaction among members of organisations, including their roles, hierarchical patterns, intercommunication, etc.; styles of organisational structure and types of leadership; the norms and cultures of organisations; decision-making in organisations; conflict resolution; relationships between formal and informal structures within organisations; interaction among organisations.

The study involves concepts and methods derived from several disciplines e.g. game theory, small group theory, systems approaches, etc. In political science it has been used mainly in the study of party organisations, committees and other small groups, and legislative bodies.

☛ GROUP BASIS OF POLITICS; ORGANISATION;
SMALL GROUP POLITICS

Outputs

☞ INPUT-OUTPUT ANALYSIS

Overload

A term employed in the communications approach to political analysis, which refers to the state of communications channels when they are used to convey messages at a rate greater than their optimum capacity. Overload, if it persists, can lead to channel failure, and perhaps the breakdown of the communications system. It is a signal for either the development of new or additional channels for information, or a reduction in the load on existing channels.

☛ COMMUNICATIONS APPROACH; POLITICAL
  COMMUNICATION; STRESS

P

Pacifism

The belief in the immorality of war, or of violence generally. Such belief had influence on the attempts to establish various forms of world government, of a consultative or judicial nature, including the League of Nations, the United Nations, and the World Court. It also frequently gives rise to problems of political obedience, when a state is at war and pacifists refuse to comply with conscription orders.

Pact

An agreement made between persons, groups or states, e.g. to formalise an alliance of some kind. It is usually used in the context of international politics, as a synonym for a treaty.

☛ TREATY

Palace revolution

A change of ruler brought about by the threat or application of force, generally by associates of the ruler or politicians with ready access to him, but usually involving an element of surprise, only the minimum of actual violence, and little or no public disturbance. It is a form of coup d'état.

☛ COUP D'ÉTAT; REVOLUTION

Panel study

The technique of using repeated interviews, or other methods of data collection, with an unchanging sample of a population, in order to study alterations in their attitudes, opinions or behaviour over a specified time period. It has been used in sociology, in social psychology, in broadcasting audience research and in market research. In political science, its best known applications have been in psephological studies, to discover changes in voting intention, and to relate these changes to other attributes of the voter, e.g. changes in his exposure to electoral propaganda, changes of occupation or residence.

☛ POPULATION; PSEPHOLOGY; SURVEY

Paradigm

A specific instance, or case, of some set of objects or phenomena under investigation, and which serves as a pattern for the study of other instances or cases by virtue of the identification and explanation of important and relevant features of that case. It is thus similar to an 'ideal type', except that a paradigm is an actual, rather than a non-existent, case. Nazi Germany might be regarded as a paradigm of totalitarianism; the Swedish example of the office could be taken as a paradigm of an Ombudsman.

☛ IDEAL TYPES

Parameters

In analysis, parameters are the dimensions or states of relevant external conditions which are held constant for any given series of tests, experiments, measurements, etc., but which are capable of being varied for other series of such tests or measurements.

☛ VARIABLES

Pareto optimum

A concept, derived from economics, used in certain types of model concerning bargaining processes. It refers to the point of equilibrium (or several such points, possibly) that exists, in a bargaining situation where A is exchanging amounts of X with B and receives amounts of Y from B, and where the maximum amount of X that A is willing to give up in exchange for another unit of Y is just equal to the minimum amount of X that B is willing to take in exchange for another unit of Y. No further exchange is possible beyond this point that would benefit both parties, though one or other party might be able to be in a more advantageous position. It is thus a likely point at which a bargain might be struck, assuming that this point can be discovered, that both parties behave 'rationally', and that no intervening factors such as coercion are present.

☛ BARGAINING THEORY

Partial theory

☞ THEORY

Participant observation

A situation in social science research where either a member of a group becomes also an observer, recording or transmitting pertinent information about the behaviour of his group, or an outsider becomes a member of the group for the same purpose.

Several advantages are served by participant observation rather than external observation or interview techniques. The situation under observation is likely to be less affected by the investigation if members of the group are unaware, or less aware, of the fact that they are being observed. The observer is capable of gaining a more sensitive notion of the group and its activities by participating in the group than if he remained external to it. However, ethical and practical problems are raised connected with the concealed 'dual role' of the participant observer.

The technique has been used mainly in anthropology, industrial, organisational and community studies in sociology, and in small group studies. Its applications in political science would be mainly in the areas of community and small group studies, decision-making and election studies.

☛ OBSERVATION

P 144

Participation

The term is usually applied to voluntary, rather than coerced, activities, though this is a distinction not necessarily inherent in the word itself.

Participation, as used in political contexts, is thus the voluntary activity of an individual in political affairs, including voting; membership and activity connected with political groups such as movements, parties, pressure groups, interests; office holding in political institutions; informal activities such as political discussion or attendance at political events; political persuasion of the authorities or members of the political public. The term is therefore closely associated with democratic political systems, in so far as non-democratic systems tend to limit participation by the general public, or to channel it in predetermined ways.

☛ MOBILISATION

Party

A political party is an organised group, made up of members who subscribe to some common set of values or policies, which has as its fundamental aim the attainment of political power and public office, generally by constitutional means, in order to implement these policies. It differs from lobbies, pressure groups and interest groups, since these are concerned with influencing government decisions or legislative proposals in some specific case, or over a limited range of cases, whereas a party seeks to implement its policies over the whole spectrum of public affairs. A party differs from a movement by virtue of its more formal organisational structure, the more specific nature of its aims, and its broad acceptance of the methods of obtaining political power that currently prevail in the system.

The exercise of governmental power is not the only function which a political party fulfils. It is an agency for political recruitment, an instrument of political socialisation, a channel for political communication, etc. In terms of the political system, it has 'gatekeeping' and interest-aggregative roles, among others.

Parties in one-party states have the same fundamental aims of the control of governmental power as do parties in competitive party systems. The sources of political competition and rivalry may differ (e.g. there may be, as there has been in Russia and China, competition from the military or the bureaucracy).

Specialised parties, and minor parties with little or no hope of acting as the government in the foreseeable future, are marginal cases within the terms of the definition outlined here. A specialised party, such as the nationalist parties of Great Britain, is perhaps better classified as a pressure group which uses electoral campaigns as a strategy; minor parties with comprehensive policies and with possibilities of sharing power in a coalition (e.g. the West German Free Democrats) clearly fall within the terms of the definition above.

Parties have been studied in many ways by political scientists, including the case study method, comparative studies, historical accounts, behavioural studies, etc. In particular, the aspects of organisational structure, leadership, recruitment methods, policies and policy-making processes, the functions and value systems, and the background and political behaviour of members and supporters have been the subjects of major studies.

☛ BLOC; COALITION; FACTION; INTEREST; LOBBY; MOVEMENT; PARTY SYSTEM; PRESSURE GROUP

Party system

A party system is the complex interrelationship between political parties, the political community, the political public and the functions which parties perform. Thus party systems vary according to the major dimensions of these components.

The number of active parties seeking political power is the most obvious of these dimensions. In some states, by law or by force of political circumstance, only one party exists (e.g. the USSR); in others there is an observable tendency toward political competition between two, and only two, major parties (e.g. the USA, the United Kingdom); in yet other states, several parties exist and persist, and governments tend to be multiparty coalitions (e.g. the three parties of West Germany, the multiparty systems of the French Fourth and Fifth Republics, Weimar Germany's many parties). Also important as a dimension of party systems is the distribution of support among the parties. In some states one or two parties will command considerable support in normal circumstances, while other parties which exist gather only minor support at elections (e.g. Sweden, Canada), and in other states several parties exist, each capable of attracting only a minor level of support (e.g. the French Fourth Republic). Relations with the political community constitute an important factor. In the one-party states of the post-Civil War period, following 'Reconstruction', the dominance of the Democratic Party was maintained by legal and politico-social sanctions, and was not the result of freely given support from a fully enfranchised population. The roles of the Nazi Party in Germany and the Communist Party in the USSR are examples of parties being involved much more directly and 'responsibly' with the organs of state power than are parties in e.g. western Europe today. Finally, the basis of party organisation should be noted. Some parties are secular coalitions based on broad acceptance of fundamental programmes, while others are very ideological, perhaps based on a religious or ethnic position, and others yet again have little interest in programme or ideology, concerning themselves more with patronage and power-seeking.

Thus party systems are complex, varied, and susceptible to influence by components of the political system, the sociocultural system, and the traditions which the political community has accumulated.

☞ POLITICAL PARTY

Patronage

The power to appoint persons to office or to nominate them for the award of honours on the basis of the opinion of the authority (e.g. prime minister, president, senator) exercising the patronage. Such power may be restricted by e.g. tradition, legislative requirements, or the necessity for confirmation of appointments by some external body (e.g. the monarch, the US Senate), but the essence of patronage is the discretionary choice available to the authority.

The term is chiefly applied to appointment to political or administrative posts, such as Cabinet office, membership of public boards, or an ambassadorship, but it also includes, in the British political system, for instance, appointments to judicial office, to certain educational posts (such as the headships of certain Oxford and Cambridge colleges), and religious appointments in the Church of England such as archbishoprics, as well as the bestowal of peerages, titles and orders of chivalry. In the American political system, patronage is widespread at the federal, state and local levels, and the president, senators, representatives, state governors, mayors, etc. all have patronage powers, though the increase in the proportion of 'non-patronage' federal civil service appointments has reduced the number of patronage posts to be filled in the federal administration.

The term 'patronage' does not in itself imply venal or corrupt use of appointive powers, though in some contexts the suggestion of improper motives is obviously involved in the choice of this word.

☞ NEPOTISM

Pattern maintenance

One of the requisite functions of social (including political) systems, identified by Talcott Parsons. It is the function of those structures, such as the family, which maintain, and transmit to members of the system, the major values of the system. It therefore involves such activities as political socialisation and social control.

☞ ACTION THEORY; STRUCTURAL-FUNCTIONAL ANALYSIS

Peer group

A group characterised by the possession of some common factor, e.g. age, educational attainment, social status, which is believed to be relevant to the values and interrelationships of members of the group. Peer group membership may, for instance, be influential in the formation of political attitudes, determination of the level of political participation, or the acceptance of various forms of authority.

☞ PRIMARY GROUP

Persistence

A political system may be said to exhibit persistence when it is able to respond to internal and environmental stresses without endangering its own identity as a system. Persistence does not rule out change; a system may still be said to be exhibiting persistence if it is developing more complex qualities, for instance. But a destruction of boundaries (e.g. by absorption by another political system) or division (e.g. by secession) are examples of a failure of persistence. Germany in 1945 is an example of such failure; the USA in the 1860s, the Congo and Nigeria more recently are examples of crises of persistence.

☞ SYSTEMS ANALYSIS

Personation

The attempt to pass oneself off as another person. In politics, personation usually concerns a fraudulent attempt to vote in place of someone else.

Pillarisation

The tendency for political life to be organised on the basis of strong fundamental social divisions, and for individuals' political behaviour to relate itself to membership of some important social group. Examples of pillarisation are: the religious denominations as factors in Dutch politics; regional-tribal divisions in Nigerian politics.

The term is used in R. Dahrendorf, *Society and Democracy in Germany*, Weidenfeld & Nicolson, 1968, pp. 116-18.

Planning

Planning is the process whereby an organisation considers its goals in the light of what is known of the future, and selects among these goals; in doing this, it generally specifies various time constraints for the achievement of its goals and indicates methods of implementation, including the allocation of appropriate resources.

It is thus a process that may be found in any subsystem of society, at any level of organisation that is possessed of a minimum autonomy in the choice of goals. Thus there is to be found, at the societal level: economic planning, defence planning, regional, urban and environmental planning, development planning, welfare planning, etc.; at the organisational levels below that of society itself: resource planning and budgeting, manpower planning, etc.

Planning is similar to policy-making, though a policy is, in various ways, more comprehensive and includes the definition of goals as well as choice among them. Thus it is false to draw distinctions between planned and unplanned social policies; the important distinction is between those societies which follow incrementalist strategies of policy-making, involving only broad and simple planning strategies, with little detail, and those which favour comprehensive and systematic planning as a guide to the implementation of policies. Though socialist and 'statist' societies are more likely to be highly reliant on planning, comprehensive plans may also be prepared by e.g. militaristic regimes or right-wing regimes, especially as contingency planning.

Development planning is a particular type of planning aimed at the deliberate growth of a society, by taking into consideration contemporaneous changes in the economic, political, administrative, technological and other subsystems of the society.

☞ POLICY ANALYSIS; POLITICAL DEVELOPMENT

Planning-Programming-Budgeting System (PPBS)

A system of public budgeting of resources, developed in the US administration in the 1960s, which focuses attention on the cost of programmes, the costs of alternatives, and the constraints of resource allocation and time which are involved in policy planning.

As applied in American government, each administrative department or agency outlines its objectives, in terms of the goods and services it supplies, or plans to provide, in the period for which the budget is produced. These objectives are translated into programmes for their attainment, costed, and compared with alternative programmes and their costs. The time dimension is emphasised, both in terms of true costs over a time period (taking into account rates of interest, etc.), and by preparing progress reports on previously budgeted programmes regarding the rate of achievement of planned objectives, and expenditures compared to planned costs.

The system thus differs from orthodox public budgeting by arranging expenditures in terms of programmes, rather than aggregate 'line items' such as staff costs, equipment, transport, etc.; and by linking political ends and economic means, rather than emphasising the one or the other as the fundamental criterion for reviewing the contents of a budget.

☞ BUDGET

Platform

A series of policy proposals produced on behalf of a candidate or party during an election campaign. It may refer to the whole of the proposals for a particular party (e.g. the Conservative Party platform) or to a section of such proposals (e.g. the civil rights platform of the Democratic Party).

A single proposal in a platform is sometimes referred to as a 'plank'.

☛ CAMPAIGN; MANIFESTO

Plebiscite

A vote by an electorate on a proposed change of regime, or to ratify such a change if it has already occurred.

Examples of plebiscites include that held in the Saar in 1935 to decide on union with Germany (and, as a *de facto* plebiscite, the Saar elections of 1955 which led to union with West Germany), and the plebiscites which conferred the status of Life Consul (1802) and Emperor (1804) on Napoleon. A referendum may be regarded as a *de facto* plebiscite by a ruler; the 1969 referendum on changes in the French Constitution was so regarded by de Gaulle in advance of the vote, and he resigned as President when his proposals for change were defeated.

☛ REFERENDUM

Pluralism

The belief that power is, or should be, distributed among many groups and interests in society, and which thus opposes the monism of those who hold that there should be in every state an ultimate, supreme source of power, i.e. some 'sovereign' body. Pluralists hold that it is morally preferable for individuals to be associated politically with a potentially diverse range of groups and interests, that these groups and interests are, historically or logically, prior to the state, and, indeed, that the state is itself composed of these groups and interests and cannot properly be conceived as distinct from them. Thus the functions of the state are of a coordinating and compromising, rather than an imposing, nature.

While pluralism may be seen as closely connected with liberalism, it is also a reaction against the extreme liberal viewpoint in which the individual is stressed as separated from the social environment in which he exists. Pluralism attempts to reintegrate the individual and his social environment, without subjecting him to the unmodified power of the state.

☛ LIBERALISM; MONISM; SOVEREIGNTY; STATE

Plurality

The proportion of votes secured by a candidate which is (*a*) more than the proportion obtained by any of the rival candidates for office, and (*b*) is less than a majority of the total votes cast, i.e. is a proportion smaller than 50 per cent plus one vote.

☛ MAJORITY

Plutocracy

The rule of the wealthy in a society. It is thus generally a form of oligarchic rule. Marxists maintain that, since wealth is created by factors of production, and control of factors of production is the basis of political rule, all forms of government have been plutocratic, but this broad view robs the concept of its utility in distinguishing plutocratic societies from e.g. military oligarchies, political systems based on caste, or elites based on educational or other selective procedures.

Many of the medieval city states were plutocracies, and it could be maintained that, if not the whole of the USA, certainly some of its states and cities in the past have been informally ruled as plutocracies.

Polarisation

The process of the clustering of several elements around one, two or several points of distribution. Thus, in international politics, the forming of alliances around two major powers (bipolarity) or several major powers (multipolarity). In psephological studies, polarisation is used as the term to describe the tendency for votes to be given in a multiparty system to the two major parties with the opportunity to form governments.

☛ BIPOLARITY; MULTIPOLARITY

Policy

A set of decisions taken by a political actor or group, concerning the selection of goals and the methods of attaining them, within a specified situation. These decisions, in principle, should be within the power of the policy-maker to achieve.

A policy may be simple—consisting, for example, of a single

decision—or it may be a complex set of contingency plans. It may be a decision to postpone decision. It may be relatively concrete (e.g. a policy to achieve a balance of payments surplus within two years), or abstract (e.g. a policy of non-intervention).

Four elements of this definition of policy require special attention. The *selection of goals* implies knowledge of the ordering of values and the value system which the policy-maker possesses. Such goals may be positive (e.g. economic growth) or negative (e.g. freedom from aggression); they may be of various levels of generality (e.g. a policy of nationalisation in general; a policy of nationalisation of major industries; a policy for the nationalisation of the steel industry). The *methods* of attaining the goals must involve human behaviour; this requirement distinguishes policy from technology (involving inanimate objects and their activity). The *specified situation* is one of future interaction between the policy-making process and the social and physical environment, which interaction imposes constraints on the attainment of goals. The element of *control* by the policy-maker may be through authority, persuasion, or coercion, but if it is not present, at least in principle, then the word 'policy' is inappropriate, and the selection of goals is merely a statement of intention.

➤ CONSTRAINT; DECISION; GOAL ATTAINMENT; POLICY ANALYSIS; POLICY APPROACH; VALUE SYSTEM

Policy analysis

Part of the interdiscipline of policy sciences, policy analysis is the study of the formation of policy, the production of policy outputs, the inputs (e.g. political support, information) that are involved in such production of policy outputs, the values of policy-makers, the environment of the policy-making system, the costs of policy alternatives (e.g. by use of budgetary techniques such as planning-programming-budgeting, normative economics, game theory, etc.) and metapolicy—the study of policies for improving policy formation.

It draws on many of the approaches and methods of political science, such as the systems approach, the policy approach, decision-making analysis and aspects of the study of political behaviour, but in addition it involves concepts and approaches from other disciplines such as economics, administrative theory and psychology.

Several books have surveyed major aspects of policy analysis; two of the most comprehensive are: Y. Dror, *Public Policymaking Reexamined*, San Francisco, Chandler, 1968, and R. Bauer and K. Gergen, eds, *The Study of Policy Formation*, New York, Free Press, 1968.

In a secondary usage, policy analysis may be used as a term referring to the detailed analytical examination of a particular policy, or policy-making system.

☛ DECISION-MAKING ANALYSIS; METAPOLICY; PLANNING-PROGRAMMING-BUDGETING SYSTEM (PPBS); POLICY; POLICY APPROACH

Policy approach

One important set of definitions of political science concentrates on the 'authoritative allocation of values for a society' (Easton), on 'who gets what, when and how' (Lasswell), on the setting of goals for society (Mitchell), the collective pursuit of collective goals (Parsons), or 'the process of making governmental policies' (A. Ranney, *The Governing of Men*, Holt, Rinehart and Winston, 1958, p. 7). Thus the policy approach involves the acceptance of some such definition of politics, concerning the formation and implementation of policy, and the analysis of political processes, institutions and behaviour in terms of their relationship to policy-making. It does not claim to be an exclusive approach, but rather one of the major approaches among several, and one which is useful for the explanation of political events.

The policy approach involves the identification of the authorities and the policy-making system of the social group under investigation, the analysis of its norms, procedures and component elements, and the recognition of those relevant actors outside the system concerned with initiating, influencing or obstructing the process of policy formation with respect to a specified policy demand. The approach thus may study, or take account of, relevant aspects of the institutions of government, elites and leadership, political groups such as parties and pressure groups, ideology as it affects the formation of policy, or its processing and acceptance, electoral behaviour, political communication, and the distribution of political power within the political system. While closely associated with the emerging discipline of policy analysis, it is distinct from it.

Examples of particular works which may be said to incorporate the policy approach include J. Christoph, *Capital Punishment and British Politics*, Allen & Unwin, 1960; H. H. Wilson, *Pressure Group: the Campaign for Commercial Television*, Secker & Warburg, 1961; F. Smallwood, *Greater London, The Politics of Metropolitan Reform*, Indianapolis, Bobbs-Merrill, 1965; L. Rainwater and W. Yancey, *The Moynihan Report and the Politics of Controversy*, Massachusetts Institute of Technology Press, 1967

☛ POLICY; POLICY ANALYSIS

Political actor

A person or group possessed of a politically relevant role, i.e. a role which affects directly the operations of some structure within the political system, however small this effect might be. Thus a voter, a committee of Congress, a dictator, the secretary of a political party branch, an assassin and a pressure group are all political actors.

Political analysis

Political analysis is the intellectual process of defining, classifying and explaining political phenomena and political problems. To undertake these tasks, it makes use of the range of concepts, methods, approaches, models, theories, etc., available at the time. It is not so much a field within political science as a major dimension of it, alongside political history, political description, and political philosophy. However, sub-areas of political analysis can be identified, both in terms of subject (e.g. policy analysis, electoral analysis, systems analysis) and in terms of the stage or method of analysis (e.g. methodology, taxonomy, theory construction, comparative analysis, mathematical analysis).

☛ METHODOLOGY; POLICY ANALYSIS; POLITICAL
   SCIENCE; SYSTEMS ANALYSIS

Political anthropology

Political anthropology includes those aspects of the study of anthropology (which is the study of the social arrangements of ethnic groups) which are concerned with the ways in which political functions are carried out in various ethnic communities. Such functions are performed by various structures in most, if not all, ethnic groups, though formal political structures may be absent. Political anthropology studies the effects of cultural tradition, the interaction of a society with its physical environment, the effects of social and technological change, and similar factors on the ways in which political structures evolve and change, and the ways in which political functions are performed. It is closely linked with the study of law and legal processes in such societies.

An example of a study in political anthropology is L. Mair, *Primitive Government*, Penguin Books, 1962.

☛ CUSTOM; POLITICAL CULTURE; POLITICS;
STRUCTURAL-FUNCTIONAL ANALYSIS

Political asylum

The practice of permitting inhabitants of some foreign territory to obtain sanctuary in the host territory, when they are in danger of punishment or other peril due to their political beliefs or actions. On rare occasions asylum may also be granted within embassies or on vessels belonging to the host country, but usually the conditions attached to the grant of asylum are more stringent in such cases.

Political behaviour

Political behaviour, as an area of study within political science, is concerned with those aspects of human behaviour that take place within political contexts, i.e. within a state or other political community, for political purposes or with political motivation. Its focus is the individual person—as voter, leader, revolutionary, party member, opinion leader, etc.—rather than the group or the political system, but it necessarily takes account of the influences of the group on the individual's behaviour, the constraints of the system on the individual's opportunities for action, and the effects of the political culture on his attitudes and political habits.

The major areas of interest for political scientists who have undertaken the study of political behaviour have been the psychological and social influences on behaviour, e.g. political socialisation; the political ideologies, attitudes and opinions of individuals, and their manifestations; the relationship between individuals as political actors and the groups to which they belong; political activity such as voting and other forms of political participation, leadership, decision-making, political violence, etc.; the methods of political communication used by individuals; and the relationship between individual behaviour and the political system and its environment. Many of these topics require, or at the very least permit, interdisciplinary and cross-disciplinary research.

It is important to distinguish 'political behaviour' as a term from the 'behavioural approach', which refers rather to a set of orientations, procedures and methods of analysis, and is not confined to the topics of individual-based political behaviour outlined above.

☛ BEHAVIOURAL APPROACH; MICRO-POLITICS; POLITICAL CULTURE; POLITICAL PSYCHOLOGY; POLITICAL SOCIALISATION; POLITICAL SYSTEM

Political communication

Political communication is the process whereby components of a political system, such as groups, institutions, individual political actors, transmit and receive information relevant to the functioning of the system. The term may also be applied to the information so transmitted and received.

The concept is by no means limited in application to persuasive communication, or propaganda; the information may be of any type, e.g. statistics, intelligence reports, statements of opinion, decisions. The motive for transmitting the information is not an important factor in determining whether it constitutes political communication; the sender, channels, content and receiver are the criteria.

Political communication may be studied in many ways. Its content may be analysed (content analysis); the relationships between communications subsystems and political systems generally may be investigated (e.g. the work of Karl Deutsch); the media of communication may be studied from various viewpoints; the functions of political communication may be identified and analysed; and so on.

☛ AUDIENCE; COMMUNICATIONS APPROACH; CONTENT ANALYSIS; FEEDBACK; PROPAGANDA

Political community

☛ COMMUNITY; COMMUNITY STUDIES; POLITY

Political culture

A political culture is the set of orientations concerning the political process (e.g. ideologies, attitudes, beliefs), and their expression, as they are related to members of a political system and set in the context of the norms of that system. Its particular form in any society is a product of the historical experiences that have affected the political system, and the results of the political socialisation processes experienced by members of the political system.

Among the dimensions or components of political culture which have been studied by political scientists are the agents and styles of political socialisation; the interrelationship between ideological and attitudinal values concerning politics, and the rules and procedures of the political system; orientations towards political leadership and the political process itself; the focus of political identity of individuals and groups.

A political culture will generally contain identifiable sub-cultures, based on e.g. religion, regional differences, ethnic groups, social status, etc. These subcultures will consist of political attitudes and values distinct from those of the general political culture with respect to particular political institutions and processes. Should these subcultures become dominant, the political integration of the community may be threatened. Examples of such subcultures which tend to dominance: the nationalist subculture in Northern Ireland, the French sub-culture in Quebec, and the Greek and Turkish subcultures in Cyprus.

A major comparative study of aspects of political culture in five democratic political systems was published as G. Almond and S. Verba, *The Civic Culture*, Princeton University Press, 1963. Also important as a contribution to the empirical study of political cultures is L. Pye and S. Verba, eds, *Political Culture and Political Development*, Princeton University Press, 1965.

☛ ATTITUDES; POLITICAL INTEGRATION; POLITICAL SOCIALISATION

Political development

The study of political development focuses on the effects of rapid social and economic change on the political arrangements of society, and the role that is played by political institutions and forces in affecting the course of developmental change. Though the area chosen for study may be a region extending over several states, or an area within a state, the study of political development is usually associated with newly independent states that were, until recently, colonies of western states, so the processes of decolonisation and achievement of political independence are especially relevant.

Among the more specific questions concerning politics that may be dealt with in the study of developmental change are the effects of economic and social change on the institutions of government and on the methods and levels of political participation; the roles of elites and styles of leadership in developing nations; the search for equality in social and political relationships; the influence of the military; the relationship between ideology and development, especially concerning nationalism, Communism and democracy; political communication and the mass media; political socialisation, and the role of education as a developmental force; the integration of minorities; the role of the bureaucracy. Several of these problems have been the subjects of volumes in the series *Studies in Political Development*, published by the Princeton University Press. Also important as a survey of political development is the series of essays edited by G. Almond and J. Coleman, *The Politics of the Developing Areas*, Princeton University Press, 1960.

A major conceptual difficulty arises over the use of the term 'development'. Notions of some predetermined course of political development which all developing states have to follow, on the model of the western democracies, or the European Communist states, are fallacious. On the other hand, scholars have distinguished several trends which appear to be associated with processes of political development, such as increased complexity and specialisation of political roles and institutions, the enlargement of an educated political elite, the increased politicisation of the population (through mass parties, for instance), the emergence of national, rather than parochial, political issues, and of the interests concerned with these issues, urbanisation, economic growth, and the increasing interrelationship of the political, social and economic spheres of society.

☛ DEVELOPMENT STUDIES; MODERNISATION

Political economy

Before the nineteenth century the term was used to refer to the study of economics in general, but almost entirely in terms of national economies. Later usage narrowed the term to refer to the study of economic policy, the linkage between political and economic factors in public policy, and related matters.

☞ ECONOMIC APPROACHES TO POLITICS

Political elites

Social groups, consisting of a small minority of the total population of a community, who exercise a predominant influence on political outcomes, by virtue of their occupancy of important political offices, their membership of influential social classes or castes, their common educational background, their membership of economic or social elite groups, etc.

☞ ELITE

Political geography

The study of the relationship between political areas, principally states, and their physical environment. It is based on the fact that the major political units of the world (empires, states, provinces, townships, colonies, etc.) are territorial areas, and are influenced by geographic factors.

Important aspects of the subject include geographical influences on the formation and political growth of states; the nature of frontiers and boundaries; the effects of geography on international relations; the structure of communications networks; administrative and regional divisions of states; demography as affected by geographic factors; the distribution of resources.

☞ APPORTIONMENT; AREA STUDIES; COUNTRY
    STUDIES; ENVIRONMENT; GEOPOLITICS;
    REGIONAL STUDIES (A): domestic regions; REGIONAL
    STUDIES (B): international regions

Political history

The study of past political systems, events, processes, institutions, actors and behaviour, that is, of the chronological dimension of political science itself. Such study includes the establishment of facts from the evidence provided by historical records, and the estimation of the causes of events through the explanation of relationships between political actors, institutions and processes. Such explanation may of necessity draw on facts regarding the effects of the environment—physical and social—on the political system.

Examples of works of political history abound, and range from the writings of L. B. Namier on eighteenth-century matters to the more recent chronicles of Theodore H. White's *Making of the President* series (Jonathan Cape). Any listing of examples would include histories focused on personalities, e.g. Trotsky's biography of Stalin, Eisenhower's autobiographies covering his presidential years; on institutions: e.g. W. E. Binkley, *American Political Parties*, 4th edn, New York, Knopf, 1963, I. Bulmer-Thomas, *The Growth of the British Party System*, 2nd edn, London, J. Baker, 1968; on events: Hugh Thomas, *The Spanish Civil War*, Eyre & Spottiswoode, 1961 and J. W. Wheeler-Bennett's *Munich: Prologue to Tragedy*, Macmillan, 1948, are examples; and on political ideologies: e.g. E. Nolte, *Three Faces of Fascism* (trans. from German), Weidenfeld & Nicolson, 1965, G. D. H. Cole, *A History of Socialist Thought*, 5 vols, Macmillan, 1952–60.

Political integration

Political integration is the state of cohesion which exists in a political community, as demonstrated by a high degree of mutual political interaction among the members of that community, based on consent rather than coercion. While distinguishable from other aspects of social integration (e.g. economic and religious integration) by this emphasis on political interaction as its basis, it is obviously closely associated with them. Political integration is part of the 'requisite function' of integration which occurs in a social system, as identified by Parsons in his writings on action theory.

The degree of integration of a community is related to several factors, including the dominance of the political culture of the community or system over the subcultures within it; the efficacy of political institutions and processes of the community in meeting expectations; the ease and frequency of political communication among members of the community, etc. Malintegration occurs when the range of shared political values is diminished, coercion becomes necessary to obtain compliance with the law, and demands are made by sections of the community for secession.

Stresses which lead to a weakening of political integration must be reduced by appropriate responses from the political authorities, otherwise the system will tend to divide, or will collapse entirely. Such stresses may result from societal change, external threat, failure to remove sources of cleavage, inability to satisfy the demands of members of some salient subculture, economic deprivation, etc. Examples of such malintegrative stress in modern history are those associated with Bavarian separatism in Germany; the 'black power' movements in the USA; Celtic nationalism in Great Britain; the attempted Biafran secession; and the departure of Singapore from the Malaysian Federation in 1965.

Some authorities (e.g. Edward Shils) have focused on the division between 'elite' and 'mass' as the major problem of political integration, but others have noted that in many states a plurality of elites exists, and malintegration is as likely to occur through a failure of consensus at elite level as between elite and mass.

Studies of political integration have included several case studies of secessionist movements; examination of the creation of federations and suprastate organisations; the political integration problems facing developing states; etc. Two major works on theoretical aspects of political integration are C. Ake, *A Theory of Political Integration*, Homewood, USA, Dorsey Press, 1967, and P. Jacob and J. Toscano, eds, *The Integration of Political Communities*, Lippincott, 1964

☛ CLEAVAGE; COHESION; CONSENSUS; POLITICAL CULTURE; POLITICAL SYSTEM; SECESSION

Political party

☛ PARTY

Political philosophy

The study of the moral and metaphysical aspects of politics, grounded almost invariably in a familiarity with the history of political thought.

Political philosophy employs the methods of philosophy and history to deal with questions of, *inter alia*, the nature of the state and of political life, the philosophic aspects of the study of politics, the grounds of political obligation, the moral qualities of different forms of government, and the relationship between morality and political policy. Thus it inevitably overlaps with other disciplines, such as ethics and social philosophy.

☛ POLITICAL THEORY; POLITICAL THOUGHT

Political psychology

Political psychology is that branch of political science that focuses on the psychological foundations of human behaviour in its political aspects and manifestations. It is based on the premise that, since political actions are, ultimately, the actions of individuals, the explanation of those actions must include psychological factors.

Political actions are concerned with the preferences that individuals have concerning competing goals and values, and methods of attaining them, and their choice of persons to represent or lead them. Political psychology assumes that such actions are directly related to the attitudes that individuals possess regarding these matters, and that such attitudes are, in part, determined by more fundamental ideological beliefs and personality styles.

Thus the interests of political psychologists include the relationships between personality factors and political behaviour; the classification and scaling of political attitudes; the processes of political learning and political socialisation; the psychological bases of leadership styles; the 'clustering' (or 'association') of political attitudes.

A comprehensive review of many of these areas is contained in H. Eysenck, *The Psychology of Politics*, Routledge & Kegan Paul, 1954. Harold Lasswell, Robert Lane and Paul Lazarsfeld are other notable names in the field.

☛ ATTITUDE SCALING; ATTITUDES; BEHAVIOURAL APPROACH; MOTIVATION; POLITICAL SOCIALISATION

Political resources

Those values possessed by political actors which are capable of being used or exchanged in order to produce desired political outcomes.

Scholars have produced various examples and classifications of political resources, but most of them seem to agree that certain personal skills and attributes (e.g. leadership skills, occupancy of political office, possession of politically relevant information), political goods (e.g. money, personnel, support, the vote in an election), time, and political outputs (e.g. policies, promulgation of decisions, actions) are major categories of political resources.

☛ ECONOMIC APPROACHES TO POLITICS

Political science

The term 'political science' has three grades of meaning. It may refer to the general discipline, i.e. the broad study of politics itself. It may be used to distinguish the study of political institutions and processes from the study of political ideas. It may refer to those aspects of the discipline that are based on empirical, rather than normative, theory, and in which the methodology is, at least in principle, 'scientifically' based with regard to replication and validation.

In its use as the title of a discipline, 'political science' refers to an imprecisely defined body of knowledge, involving the study of political ideas, institutions, processes and events, mainly—some would say entirely—concerned with the government of states. Historically, this body of knowledge has relied more on tradition than on any logical principle of exclusion to define what does, and what does not, belong within the discipline. Thus aspects of constitutional, public, and international law, history, ethics, philosophy, public administration, anthropology, and many other subjects were included in so far as they bore some relevance to political events, notions of citizenship and good government, the exercise of political power and the workings of political institutions. In most universities, at least in Europe and the Commonwealth, departments of political science would not exclude any of these aspects of political study.

The term is sometimes employed as a synonym for the study of government, as distinct from the study of political ideas, though in this usage it would include the effects of political ideas in so far as they appeared to influence the policies and activities of the political institutions under study, e.g. Bolshevism as an influence on the Russian revolutions of 1917, socialism as an influence within the British Labour Party, the effects of civil rights ideas on the policies of the Kennedy administration.

The use of the term in its most specific form, to refer to the empirical aspects of the discipline, based on scientific method, involves also the argument over how far, or even whether, politics can be studied as a science, and the criticisms that have been made over the dangers of 'scientism'. A well-known indictment of some of these dangers in the American context is B. Crick, *The American Science of Politics*, Routledge & Kegan Paul, 1959. Some counterarguments to critics of the scientific approach are summarised in D. Easton, *The Political System*, New York, Knopf, 1953. But in so far as politics claims to be included in the ranks of the social sciences, it must expect its work to be judged by the same standards of scientific validity that are applied to economics, psychology, sociology and related disciplines. Thus it must attempt to discover, test and refine hypotheses, and construct at least valid partial theories, even if the search for a general theory is at present a utopian endeavour.

☛ GENERAL THEORY; GOVERNMENT (B): study area; PARTIAL THEORY; POLITICAL PHILOSOPHY; POLITICAL THEORY; POLITICS; SCIENTIFIC METHOD

Political socialisation

Political socialisation is the process whereby, on the one hand, an individual acquires attitudes and orientations towards political phenomena, and, on the other hand, whereby society transmits political norms and beliefs from one generation to the next. These two aspects—various authorities have stressed one more than the other—may be in contradiction where an individual has apparently acquired deviant attitudes and orientations.

The socialisation process tends to be gradual and to extend from early childhood into adulthood. It appears that basic political attitudes are acquired first: loyalty toward the society (or race, nation, state, etc.), recognition of authority, and predispositions towards its exercise; then come more specific attitudes such as broad identification with a political party; then attitudes that may be as specific as a stance on some particular policy or programme. While this process normally occurs in sequence through the life of an individual, major societal changes or his entry into a new society (e.g. through emigration) may involve a new socialisation process at a relatively late age.

Political socialisation can occur through direct or indirect processes. Among these are: personal political experiences, imitation, political education, participation in non-political situations which may involve, e.g. decision-making or authority relationships, the transfer of non-political socialisation to political situations (e.g. general social attitudes such as social efficacy), and information from e.g. the mass media.

The agencies of political socialisation include: the family, peer groups (e.g. gangs, small work groups), educational institutions, and large groups, both political (e.g. political parties) and non-political (e.g. churches).

The attitudes and values of these various agencies change in content and direction over time, and may well be dissimilar relative to each other. Thus an individual may experience problems of reconciling the socialisation processes to which he is submitted, e.g. working-class university graduates; rural inhabitants of modernising societies on taking up residence in a city; immigrants from a traditional culture on moving into an industrialised society.

The standard work on the subject of political socialisation is H. Hyman, *Political Socialization*, New York, Free Press, 1959. Among other political scientists who have produced major studies of relevance to political socialisation are: David Easton and Jack Dennis, R. E. Dawson, F. Greenstein, Erik Erickson, and G. Almond and S. Verba.

☛ POLITICAL BEHAVIOUR; POLITICAL CULTURE

Political sociology

The definition of the field of political sociology has long been a matter of dispute; some define it by its content in terms of the major studies produced to date; political scientists see it as the study of the effects of the social environment on the political subsystem, while sociologists are more inclined to describe it in terms of the interrelationships of political and social institutions. Though these two latter viewpoints are distinct, and would affect, for example, the frameworks and concepts used in the study of political sociology, it is likely that ultimately the same phenomena would be analysed by such study.

A concise statement of the sociologists' definition is to be found in L. Coser, ed., *Political Sociology*, Harper, 1967, p. 1, where the editor commences his introduction:

'Political sociology is that branch of sociology which is concerned with the social causes and consequences of given power distributions within or between societies, and with the social and political conflicts that lead to changes in the allocation of power.'

Studies that fall within this definition include those that concentrate on political consensus and cleavage and their social causes, the relations between social structure and political power, the analysis of elites, the social bases of political groups such as parties and pressure groups, the relationship between social and political change, the social bases of political ideologies and the influences of social institutions on political behaviour (e.g. political socialisation, political participation).

The political scientist would define political sociology as that branch of political science that deals with the interrelationships between the political subsystem and the other subsystems of society, but particularly as they affect the political subsystem (his primary concern) rather than the social system as a whole (the primary concern of the sociologist). Thus his interests would focus on the social causes of political ideology differences, the effects of social change on political institutions and policies, the social bases of voting behaviour and party membership, problems of political culture, political integration, and social causes of political stress e.g. revolutions, civil war, military interventions in politics. In summary, he would hope that such studies would explain certain political phenomena, whereas the sociologist would more probably cast his explanations in terms of the wider phenomena of society, in which political power, for instance, was just one element, perhaps analytically equal with e.g. economic power or religious power.

☛ POLITICAL ANALYSIS; POLITICAL SCIENCE

Political system

A political system is a set of structures, processes and institutions which interact with each other, and, across the boundaries of the system, with the environment, to 'allocate values authoritatively for a society' (Easton), to attain the goals of society (Parsons), and generally to perform those functions which may be defined as political. It is, conceptually, itself a subsystem of the wider societal system, such as a state, the international system, a political party, a trade union, or a tribe. It is usually regarded as an open system, involved in exchanges with its environment, and an adaptive system, capable of adaptation to changing circumstances, regulation of its own components, response to stress and, through feedback mechanisms, able to adjust its outputs to input conditions.

☛ ADAPTATION; ENVIRONMENT; INPUT-OUTPUT
ANALYSIS; PROCESS; STRUCTURE; SYSTEMS ANALYSIS

Political theory

The term is usually applied to those areas of the study of politics otherwise termed political philosophy and empirical political analysis. Political philosophy is concerned with the study of the normative and ethical aspects of political problems, the philosophic aspects of the processes by which political data or phenomena are studied, and the historical and contemporary study of political thought. Empirical political analysis involves the attempt to construct empirically based theories about political systems, political processes and political behaviour. Such theories are built up by the means of description of political phenomena, their classification, hypothesis-testing, the establishment of laws about political behaviour, etc., and are justified (in contrast to normative or prescriptive theories) by reference to observable experience and objective data, rather than appeals to divine or other abstract sources.

☛ POLITICAL ANALYSIS; POLITICAL PHILOSOPHY; POLITICAL THOUGHT; THEORY

Political thought

The area of political philosophy concerned with the study of the ideas and philosophic systems of those thinkers held to be important, on grounds of their interest, influence, relevance, etc., in relation to the development of politics as a practice or a study. Though these topics are generally studied historically, contemporary thought is a major branch of the subject. Political thought is usually approached in one of two ways: either as the study of important thinkers, e.g. Aristotle, Hobbes, Rousseau, Marx; or as the study of the development of important concepts, e.g. natural law, democracy, nationalism, socialism, sovereignty.

Political thought is often taken as an equivalent term to political philosophy, though in fact it omits the study of philosophic problems in its concentration on thinkers and their ideas, or to political theory, though it has little interest in the development of empirical or analytic theories.

☛ POLITICAL PHILOSOPHY; POLITICAL THEORY

Politicisation

Politicisation is the process of drawing into political activity, if only temporarily, groups or individuals previously uninterested in politics. In other contexts, it can refer to the process of making an issue a matter for political determination, rather than e.g.

social or economic determination; an issue or question is depoliti-cised when it is no longer regarded as a matter for political debate and decision (e.g. religion in Britain today).

☞ APATHY

Politics

The word refers both to an activity, and to the study of that activity.

As an activity, politics is the process in a social system—not necessarily confined to the level of the national state—by which the goals of that system are selected, ordered in terms of priority both temporally and concerning resource allocation, and imple-mented. It thus involves both cooperation and the resolution of conflict, by means of the exercise of political authority and, if necessary, coercion. Politics usually involves the activities of groups of various kinds, including sometimes groups of a specifically political type, such as political parties. It is disting-uished from other social processes by its concern with the 'public' goals of the society; whereas economics may be concerned with public or private allocation of resources, and social processes of a non-political nature with non-public activities.

The study of politics—including political science, political history and political philosophy—attempts to describe, classify, analyse and explain political activity and the values which are implemented by political decisions. This study is also sometimes termed 'government', but this is normally the title of a more restricted field of study, namely the politics of formal institutions at the level of the state.

☞ GOVERNMENT (B): study area; POLITICAL ANALYSIS;
  POLITICAL PHILOSOPHY; POLITICAL SCIENCE

Polity

A politically organised society, regardless of its form of govern-ment. The word usually refers to the civil organisation of a state, but may also refer to an empire, an international political com-munity, a township, etc.

☞ SOCIETY; STATE

Poll

A poll is a process for obtaining opinions. This may be done by means of a formal ballot (e.g. an election, a referendum), or by means of a survey based on questionnaires and interviews (sometimes called an 'opinion poll').

A derived meaning of 'poll' as the place where voting takes place is found in contexts such as 'half the voters went to the polls before noon'.

☞ ELECTION; VOTING

Population

The total number of persons living in a particular area, such as a town or a state.

Also, in statistics, the total number of persons (or other items) from which, for example, a sample is drawn for the purposes of a sample survey.

☞ DEMOGRAPHY; SAMPLE

Populism

An ideology of a movement or political party, often led by members of the intelligentsia, which sought the return of governmental powers from what were seen as centralised, urban-oriented oligarchies, to the common people, and particularly to those in rural areas since they were deemed to embody a simpler, more desirable way of life, based on traditional practices.

Populist movements were found in many countries, mainly in the nineteenth and twentieth centuries, generally in reaction against the stresses of technological change and the disruptions of economic and political life that accompanied such change. Examples of populism can be found in the USA, Russia, central and eastern Europe, Latin America and Asia. The United States 'People's Party' was the most highly organised expression of American populism, and in its programmes, between its 1891 first national convention and its division in 1900, stressed bimetallism, close government regulation of the railroads, a national agricultural policy based on government aid, and several political reforms such as direct election of senators. The Russian Populist movement was marked by attempts on the part of the young revolutionaries from the cities to live with the peasants, learning from them the basic socialist virtues of rural communal life, and inspiring them to revolution.

A collection of essays on various aspects of populism, including attempts at definition, is G. Ionescu and E. Gellner, eds., *Populism: its meanings and national characteristics*, Weidenfeld & Nicolson, 1969.

☛ IDEOLOGY; MOVEMENT

Power

A variety of definitions of power as a phenomenon in social relations exists, though all of them recognise the importance of the concept for the understanding of social behaviour.

Central to many definitions is the notion that power involves the ability of a person or group to affect the behaviour of other individuals or groups in specified ways, by the threat or imposition of some form of sanctions. There is disagreement over whether power is an attribute of itself, e.g. whether one can, properly, speak of a 'powerful man' without further qualification, or whether power must be defined as a relationship of the form 'X is powerful over Y, under these particular conditions, and at this time'.

The distinction between power and influence seems to reside in the relative uncertainty or certainty with which an action may be said to have been affected by the exercise of power, whereas in the exercise of influence there is always some alternative form of action open to the person subjected to influence, which in any case is often in competition with other influences. Authority is one of the sources of political power, being the ability to secure compliance on grounds of the legitimate embodiment of accepted basic values by the person exercising authority.

Political power, social power, economic power, religious power, etc., are distinguished by the set of relationships within society (or the 'subsystem') within which they operate. They may also refer to the source of the sanctions which may be called into operation by the person exercising power, e.g. a person may, by virtue of possession of economic resources, exercise power over the political actions of others.

No satisfactory method of measuring power, or of deciding on the basis of quantifiable criteria as to which of two or more opposing sources of power in a given situation will be successful, has yet been produced. However, concepts of power resources, costs of exercising power, and the transferability of e.g. political power into economic power, have been explored.

Power is sometimes taken to be the core concept of the study of politics, involving consideration of its distribution and institutionalisation, questions of sovereignty, the settlement of the exercise of power in conflicting directions, the sources and methods of the legitimation of power, its maintenance and uses, etc. Many of these aspects are discussed in the readings in R. Bell, D. Edwards, and R. Wagner, eds., *Political Power: a reader in theory and research*, New York, Free Press, 1969.

☞ AUTHORITY; COERCION; INFLUENCE

Pragmatism

The claim that practice, or practical results, rather than doctrine or ideology, should be used both as a guide to the analysis of problems (e.g. in politics), and as the criterion for testing the validity and utility of theoretical and analytical ideas.

Precedent

A previous decision or action which is used as a guide or model, whether of a binding nature as in legal or administrative practice, or of an advisory type, as in various areas of political practice, in order to shape a current decision or action.

Thus, in constitutional law, a previously decided case may be taken as setting a precedent for a current case; in the civil service a decision in the past may be used as a persuasive precedent for settling a similar matter now pending; in the legislature, a matter of procedure may be settled by taking a similar past matter as a guiding precedent, etc. The important aspect of all these examples is the close similarity of the previous matter which is taken as the precedent to the current issue.

Prediction

The activity of making statements about the future. In social science this is regarded as being one of the purposes of analysis and explanation. Whereas in certain areas of social science (e.g. voting turnout, traffic accident rates, demographic trends) predictions can be made with high levels of precision and accuracy, the complexity of interacting factors plus the basically unpredictable nature of individual human behaviour make scientific prediction more difficult in social sciences.

In political science predictions may be based on several types of evidence, including intuition, the operation of a theoretical model, the extrapolation of observed trends into the future, and the use of sample survey data. The best-known area of political prediction is psephology.

Prerogative

The collection of customary powers enjoyed by a ruler (e.g. a monarch) which are subject to no formal check or veto, nor to surveillance by the courts, though in practice in a constitutional state such powers, if exercised arbitrarily, would almost invariably lead to political difficulties.

Prerogative powers may, in effect, be transferred to other persons, e.g. many of the prerogative powers of the British monarchy are now exercised by the Prime Minister.

☛ MONARCHY

Pressure group

An organised group which has as one of its purposes the exercise of influence (or 'pressure') on political institutions, for the purpose of securing favourable decisions or preventing unfavourable decisions.

Compared to a political party, the major distinguishing features of a pressure group are: the restricted range of policies with which it is concerned, compared to the universal concern of a political party; the rarity with which it contests public elections in its own name, and then only as a method of exercising political influence; its intention of exercising influence, whereas a political party seeks to exercise power. But some organisations are on the margin, exhibiting features both of a political party and of a pressure group.

A pressure group, often termed an 'interest group', differs from a lobby, which has the sole purpose of influencing legislation or the execution of policy. A pressure group generally has other purposes, such as providing services and news for its members and acting as an information and public relations organisation.

It differs from an 'interest' in so far as it is organised, whereas an interest (e.g. consumers, teenagers, old age pensioners) may be unorganised yet politically influential.

The main targets of pressure group activity will vary according to the political system concerned. Where the power of the legislature is strong relative to that of the executive, it will be subject to greater and more varied types of influence than where a strong executive dominance exists (cf. the US Senate with the British House of Commons). The degree of party discipline within the legislature is also an important factor, as strong party discipline lessens the opportunity for pressure groups to success-fully exercise influence on legislators. Occasionally the judiciary may also become a target for pressure group activity, especially where judicial interpretation or judicial review has political significance. An example is the campaign for civil rights con-ducted through the US courts by the National Association for the Advancement of Coloured People. In totalitarian systems pressure groups will be weak or non-existent, as extra-party political activity is forbidden. But in such systems interests have considerable influence (e.g. the Army in the USSR).

Methods of pressure group activity will also vary, and will depend on the opportunities afforded for 'access' to political decision-makers. Among methods found in most industrialised states are: public meetings and demonstrations, debates, special publications, personal letters to politicians, letters to the press, committee negotiations, petitions, deputations, the election of sympathetic candidates or the recruitment of existing legislators, cooperation (or its refusal) with official institutions, and various types of participation in elections.

☛ ACCESS; INTEREST; INTEREST GROUP; LOBBY;
   POLITICAL PARTY

Primary election

A preliminary election for the purpose of selecting a candidate for a political party to stand as that party's nominee in the main election. Primaries may be entirely organised by the party concern-ed, or may be controlled by public law and subjected to restric-tions in the same manner as in a public election. The question of who is qualified to vote in any primary is a matter for party rules, and, in some cases, public law.

Primaries are associated mainly with the electoral systems of the states of the USA.

☛ CANDIDATE; ELECTION

Primary group

A group, often of a relatively small size, characterised by frequent and intimate intercommunication and interaction, often based on face-to-face contact, in which members identify with the group in terms of their total personality, rather than with respect to some specialised role only. The family, peer groups, work gangs, and small committees are examples of primary groups.

☛ PEER GROUP; SECONDARY GROUP; SMALL GROUP POLITICS

Prisoners' dilemma

A special type of game within game theory, in which rational selection of strategies may be less profitable than non-rational selection, under certain assumptions.

The scenario of the game usually centres around two prisoners, who are held in separate cells, unable to communicate with each other. The prosecutor requires a confession to convict them on the original charge, but has evidence to secure conviction on a very minor charge. He promises each prisoner the following: if he confesses, and his partner does not, he will get a very light sentence; if both confess, there will be a moderate sentence for each; if he does not confess, but his partner does, he will get a heavy sentence; if neither confesses, the light sentence for the minor charge will be imposed. The game can be represented thus:

		Prisoner A	
		No confession	Confession
Prisoner B	No confession	$(1,1,)$	$(\frac{1}{2},7,)$
	Confession	$(7,\frac{1}{2},)$	$(3,3,)$

(pay-offs to A, B, in terms of years of imprisonment)

Because this is a non-zero-sum game, there is no single rational solution. If both prisoners trust each other, both will benefit more than if both confess, but there is a high risk in not confessing that one's partner will confess, thus increasing one's own penalty.

Such a game is applicable in politics to many situations, including cease-fire negotiations or armistice talks between two enemy states.

☛ GAME THEORY

Process

Sets of interactions among components of a system; processes are therefore to be found in all social systems, including political systems.

Political processes are sets of interactions concerned with such activities as the competition for political power (e.g. the electoral process), the resolution of conflict concerning the selection of political goals, or the means of achieving those goals (e.g. the bargaining process), the making of policies and the provision of rules for their implementation (e.g. the legislative process, the policy-making process).

Since each process, to the extent that it is relatively permanent, involves identifiable structures, functions and goals, each may be termed a subsystem of the political system, and analysed as such.

☛ POLITICAL SYSTEM; STRUCTURAL-FUNCTIONAL ANALYSIS

Propaganda

Persuasive communication, by means of any or all available media, designed to change or reinforce opinions on certain topics held by its audience in predetermined directions, particularly through emphasis on emotional rather than objective messages. Some authorities would include in a definition of propaganda the idea that it should be directed towards the stimulation of action as well as reinforcement or alteration of opinions.

☛ AUDIENCE; POLITICAL COMMUNICATION

Proportional representation

A system of voting designed to produce a result which reflects as accurately as possible the proportional support given to some specified characteristic of the candidates (usually party affiliation, in a national election).

In national elections, it is generally based on multimember constituencies of between about half-a-dozen and a dozen seats, or on a single, nationwide constituency. Most proportional systems involve the use of party lists, or of the single transferable vote system. The larger the constituency, in terms of the number of seats to be filled, the more exact the equation between share of the vote and share of the seats which each party will obtain.

Proportional representation tends to preserve the divisions of party groups existing at the time of its introduction, though the evidence to show that it increases the number of parties represented is not convincing. In any case, the electoral system is only one factor among many which influence the number of viable parties in a political system.

States which employ a system of proportional representation include Denmark; Eire; the Federal Republic of Germany; Israel; Sweden.

☛ D'HONDT METHOD; DROOP QUOTA; ELECTORAL QUOTA; ELECTORAL SYSTEM; HARE SYSTEM; LIST SYSTEM; PARTY SYSTEM; SINGLE TRANSFERABLE VOTE SYSTEM

Protectorate

A territory possessing, in international law, some of the attributes of independent statehood, but which is in other respects subordinate to a 'protecting' power. This subordination is especially concerned with the foreign relations of the protected state. The relationship between the protecting and the protected state is generally regulated by a treaty between them: a fact which underlines the original independent status of the protected state.

☛ ANNEXATION; COLONY; COMMONWEALTH; IMPERIALISM; STATE; TREATY

Proxy

A person authorised to vote in place of another, generally according to the previously expressed wish of the absent person.

The term is also applied to the vote itself.

☛ DELEGATE

Psephology

The study of voting and elections, particularly with regard to quantifiable factors.

Psephology is one of the most highly developed areas in political science, and one that—alongside political parties—constitutes perhaps the largest single section of the academic journals and political science shelves of libraries. For the enthusiasm with which elections and voting have been studied there are at least three explanations. First, elections are events which are discrete and dramatic, possessing an atmosphere of crisis even at a local level. Second, they constitute the area of academic political study which most readily links up with popular journalism and broadcasting, and thus with the interests of the general public in the political process. Since voting is, for many adults, the one overt act of political participation which they make, they may feel involved in it in a way they will not so readily feel about e.g. international politics, the legislative process, or problems of elites. Third and most important, elections offer readily definable and uniform units for study over a fairly lengthy time-span, and are capable of statistical and comparative analysis.

The information for psephological studies is obtained chiefly from official published sources—though the complexity and detail with which these are given vary from country to country, e.g. in the United Kingdom only gross constituency figures are given, in the USA precinct and town figures are available, in West Germany one can obtain even breakdowns by age, sex and religious affiliation—and from sample surveys, including those conducted by professional opinion research enterprises such as Gallup (UK, USA), Roper (USA), EMNID (West Germany) and National Opinion Polls (UK). Various forms of statistical analysis are then used to extract meaningful relationships, to derive classifications and to evolve theories. Examples of important works of a psephological nature include the Nuffield Series of studies of British general elections from 1945, *The American Voter*, Wiley, 1960, by A. Campbell and other members of the Survey Research Centre, University of Michigan, and *Elections and the Political Order*, Wiley, 1966, by the same authors.

☛ ELECTION; VOTING

Public administration

Broadly, public administration as an academic study is concerned with the administrative institutions and activities of government. It interests itself in the institutions which execute the decisions of the legislative and judicial branches of government, the methods and arrangements employed by such administrative institutions, and the relationships between the legislative and judicial and the administrative branches. In most developed political systems, the chief agencies of public administration are the civil service, local government bodies, independent agencies and ancillary bodies such as nationalised industries.

The distinction between 'public' and 'private' administration rests on the focus of responsibility rather than on method. Public administration is undertaken on behalf of state institutions only; private administration is an activity on behalf of a non-governmental institution such as a commercial enterprise, a political party, a charity or a religious body. While certain problems are specific to public administration as a subject of study (e.g. questions of tenure on a change of government, responsibility for policy decisions), many others are of common concern to the study of any type of administration (e.g. delegation, the use of specialists, methods of internal communication).

The differentiation of 'politics' from 'administration' is one of theoretical convenience rather than practical relevance. Many of the aspects of public administration of interest to the political scientist centre on the 'politics' of selecting from among alternative administrative solutions to problems, or alternative patterns of organisation of administrative agencies. The activity of public administration is intermeshed with politics at most of its stages, and is closely related to policy-making, for example in legislative drafting or in connection with delegated legislative powers.

Among the core problems of public administration are: the organisation and control of administrative services; the recruitment, training and promotion of personnel; budgeting and planning of resource allocation; executive-legislative relations; and problems of bureaucracy.

☞ ADMINISTRATION; BUREAUCRACY; DELEGATED LEGISLATION; EXECUTIVE; POLICY

Public opinion

Public opinion is difficult to distinguish, as a concept, from opinion in general, but the main distinction lies in the meaning given to the term 'public'. First, the 'public' itself must be defined, and such definition usually includes some indication of shared norms, and membership of a single community (nation, state, society, etc.); second, the 'public' hold the opinion in question, thus one does not talk of the opinion of the government, as government, as being 'public opinion', nor is there any meaningful way of aggregating opinions of e.g. Russians and

Americans as part of a single 'public'; thirdly, for some authorities (e.g. V. O. Key, jr) public opinion is opinion about public, rather than private, matters e.g. government policy, election issues, international relations.

Other writers have developed more sophisticated definitions, which include not only 'public' opinion on 'public matters', but also the ways it is produced, e.g. by social interaction, involving communication structures, feedback, etc., and its mobilisation through opinion groups, with goals related to the matters under dispute. (For a discussion of these definitional problems, see C. Schettler, *Public Opinion in American Society*, Harper, 1960, ch. 1).

☛ CONSENSUS; OPINION

Purge

A process by which members of a group (e.g. a political party, a legislature, a committee) are expelled on the grounds that their actions or opinions have been judged undesirable or even treacherous by the group itself, its leadership, or some important subgroup. Such expulsion is generally justified as necessary to preserve the values of the group. The purge may be accompanied by the use of court proceedings, executions, or other sanctions.

Though usually associated with the politics of authoritarian, especially totalitarian, states, purges are not found only in such regimes. Hitler's actions against the SA in 1934, various purges initiated by Stalin in the USSR, and the changes in the leadership of the Czechoslovakian Communist party following the invasion by Russia in 1968, are all examples.

Putsch

An attempt to seize political power by violent and illegal means, often involving elements of the armed forces, on the basis of a secret plot.

The 'Kapp Putsch' in Germany (1920) and the putsch involving Hitler and Ludendorff in Bavaria (1923) were unsuccessful examples; the Egyptian officers' putsch (1952) was a successful example.

☛ CIVIL-MILITARY RELATIONS; COUP D'ÉTAT;
   REBELLION; REVOLUTION

Q

Quantitative approaches

☞ MATHEMATICAL ANALYSIS; STATISTICAL ANALYSIS

Questionnaire

A series of standardised questions for use in e.g. sample surveys, panel studies, depth interviews and similar forms of inquiry. The questions may be 'open-ended', allowing absolutely free response, or 'closed-ended', permitting only a choice of response from a limited and pre-selected set of answers.

A questionnaire generally provides for the recording of answers (though this recording may be performed by other means, e.g. a tape-recorder) either by the interviewer, an assistant, or—with self-administered questionnaires—by the respondent. In addition, it will allow for the recording of specified data concerning the respondent (e.g. name, age, social class, occupation), and the interview situation (e.g. date, time and place of the administration of the questionnaire).

The design of the questionnaire is a critical factor, as poor design may affect the reliability of results obtained from its use. In particular the wording of questions, the use of internal consistency check questions, and the calculation of optimum length of interview time are all important.

☞ DEPTH INTERVIEW; INTERVIEW; PANEL STUDY; RESPONSE; SURVEY

Quorum

A specified minimum number of members of a political body necessary to be in attendance in order to constitute a session of that body. In the British House of Commons the quorum is forty; in the House of Lords it is three; in the US Senate and House of Representatives a simple majority is required in each case.

In some cases a session may continue with some lesser number present unless the quorum is challenged (a procedure which, as in the German *Bundestag*, may be restricted by certain conditions); in the event of a challenge a count must be taken.

R

··

Radicalism

An orientation found in alliance with many diverse types of ideology. Radicalism asserts the superior importance of some programme or policy, and rejects the existing traditional or procedural restrictions on the achievement of that programme or policy, often claiming that any means will be justified by the attainment of the end. Indeed, for many radicals the deliberate rejection of compromise or conciliation, of existing constraints on the achievement of their goals, of traditional political procedures, is itself valuable as part of an overall strategy.

Radicalism can be an attitude of right-wing, left-wing or centrist ideologies. Examples of radical parties or movements include: the Jacobins of revolutionary France, the radical reform movements of early nineteenth century England, the German Nazi party, the McCarthy anti-Communist movement in the USA, and some of the more extreme groups within the negro civil rights movement in the USA and the student movements in Europe and America.

☛ IDEOLOGY; MOVEMENT; POPULISM

Random sample

☞ SAMPLE

Reapportionment

The process of revising the boundaries of electoral areas or other forms of constituency, and, if necessary, altering the numbers of such constituencies. It is sometimes referred to as 'redistricting', though in Britain the word 'redistribution' is more usual.

☛ APPORTIONMENT; CONSTITUENCY

Rebellion

Open resistance to the authority and commands of a ruler or government. It may take the form of civil war or revolution if it persists and grows.

☛ CIVIL DISOBEDIENCE; CIVIL WAR; INSURRECTION; REVOLUTION

Recall (A): the institution

A device by which the electorate can terminate the period of office of an incumbent prior to the date of conclusion laid down in a constitution or by legislation. Along with such devices as referenda and legislative initiative, it is thus a method of mediating indirect democracy through elected representatives by allowing the electorate certain direct powers.

Generally, recall is required to be preceded by a petition from a minimum number or fraction of the qualified electorate, produced within a given time period. If this is complied with, a recall election is then held, to decide whether to terminate the incumbancy of the office-holder in question, and, if so, who to elect in his stead.

It is a device contained in many local authority, and some state, constitutions in the USA; it was found in various forms in the Athenian and Roman political systems; some Swiss cantons have devices for dissolving the legislature by a recall vote.

☛ DIRECT DEMOCRACY

Recall (B): remembrance

The ability to remember events or attitudes from the past. The term is employed in politics principally to refer to the ability of respondents to reply to questions in surveys regarding their opinions, attitudes, activities, etc., at some past time.

☞ RESPONSE; SURVEY

Recruitment

The process by which political groups obtain members, as either additions to the group or as replacements for other members. Such processes may include personal contact and persuasion, initiation ceremonies, formal examinations, election, cooption, appointment and promotion. Recruitment processes are of interest in connection with the study of elites, leadership groups, bureaucratic organisations, political parties, interest groups, etc.

Redistribution

☞ REAPPORTIONMENT

Redistricting

☞ REAPPORTIONMENT

Reductionist theories

Theories which attempt to simplify the explanation of some type of social phenomena by reference to existing explanations which have been produced in relation to other phenomena, social or physical. Determinist theories are examples of reductionist theories in many cases, as are theories which propose e.g. that all political phenomena are explicable by use of the theories of, say, economic, or psychological knowledge.

☞ DETERMINISM

Referendum

A vote by an electorate of a state or other political unit on a specific policy proposal, or on the ratification or amendment of a constitution, as provided for in the constitution of the political organisation concerned. Some policies (e.g. to increase the public debt by bond issues, amendments to the constitution) may require compulsory decision by a referendum, in other cases it may be used at the option of some proportion of the legislature, or on the demand of a specified minimum number of voters, as indicated by petitions.

Examples of the provision for referenda may be found in the constitutions of the Fifth French Republic, many of the states of the USA, and in some cantons of the Swiss Federation.

☛ PLEBISCITE

Regime

A regime is the term used to refer to the particular form of government which is possessed by a polity, e.g. parliamentary, totalitarian, republican. The classification of regimes according to various principles has long been a primary task of political analysis. Plato, Aristotle and Macchiavelli among the classical philosophers, Marx, Lipset and Crick among more modern political scholars have all produced their own typologies. These have drawn on such criteria as the number of effective participants in political rule; the stability of the regime; the economic system of the regime; and the attitudes of the authorities to law and politics.

David Easton, in *A Systems Analysis of Political Life* (Wiley 1965), distinguishes the regime (as meaning a style of government, and a particular set of procedures and arrangements) from the authorities who constitute the government at any particular time. Thus the authorities can be changed by peaceful means, but a regime is only changed by some form of revolutionary upheaval.

Regional studies (A): domestic regions

The study of the major subdivisions of a state, as defined geographically, including the study of their political characteristics.

A domestic region is a subdivision of a state, which possesses geographical, as well as some degree of social and economic, unity. It will generally be found to contain one or more urban centres, which act as focal points for the region in terms of commerce, employment, culture, government, communications, etc. More particularly, attempts to subdivide a state into political regions, however, on the basis of such unity encounter various problems of boundary definition, especially if several types of administrative region (e.g. for statistical purposes, or for the administration of public services) exist already. These existing boundaries may well not coincide either with each other or with other types of regional boundaries (e.g. for the circulation of local newspapers, the broadcasting of regional programmes, or public transport networks).

☛ LOCAL GOVERNMENT STUDIES; POLITICAL GEOGRAPHY; REGIONAL STUDIES (B): international regions; REGIONALISM

Regional studies (B): international regions

The intensive study of certain aspects (including political aspects) of a group of geographically contiguous states which are linked by some relevant factor such as common membership of a political or economic association (e.g. the Warsaw Pact or the Central American Common Market), or possession of a common linguistic or cultural background (e.g. Scandinavia, Latin America).

☛ AREA STUDIES; COMPARATIVE ANALYSIS; POLITICAL GEOGRAPHY; REGIONAL STUDIES (A): domestic regions

Regionalism

The belief that certain desired values would best be attained by the division of a state into distinct geographical regions, either for the general purposes of government or for some more specific purpose. Such division is often desired in terms of legislative as well as of executive powers. Regionalism also refers to policies designed to implement such a belief.

☛ DECENTRALISATION; DEVOLUTION; FEDERATION; REGIONAL STUDIES (A): domestic regions

Regulation (A): control

The term used in various forms of systems analysis to refer to the adjustments made by occupants of control positions in the system, in order to cope with stress, or to anticipate it. Thus regulative responses are one form of response to stress on the system; other responses include the operation of self-adjusting processes, relying on feedback mechanisms, or unregulated responses of structures in the system.

Thus a political threat from a foreign country could be regarded as stress, to which the system responds by a regulated action (e.g. a diplomatic communication), a self-adjusting process (e.g. a decline in tourist travel to the threatening country from the threatened country) or an unregulated response (e.g. a ban by trade unions on the handling or sale of goods from the threatening country).

☛ REGULATION (B): rule; RESPONSE; STRESS

Regulation (B): rule

A rule or statement, often governing procedures, that has the force of law in some group context. It is a term frequently used to refer to rules made by the executive branch of government, under delegated powers from the legislature.

☛ DELEGATED LEGISLATION; LAW (B): stipulative law; REGULATION (A): control

Reification

The process of mentally giving concrete reality to some abstract concept, e.g. in politics to such concepts as 'the state' or 'the nation'.

Replication

The act of repeating or duplicating a set of procedures; hence, in social science, the duplication of a previous experiment, as a means of checking the validity of procedures, results, or both.

☛ EXPERIMENT; VALIDATION

Representation

The concept of one person or group having the ability or the obligation to speak and act on behalf of a larger number of other persons or groups, e.g. in a legislature, at a party convention, in negotiations within a committee.

The basis of representation may vary considerably. One

method is simple election by those to be represented (as in all competitive legislative elections, or in the election of the Speaker of the House of Commons, the Speaker of the House of Representatives, the President of the Bundestag). Another is the choice of a representative who is, in some essential feature or quality, typical of those to be represented (as in the nomination of members of certain public boards in Britain and the USA). Representation may be carried to the point of delegation, when the representative lacks all discretion as to the way he votes or the case he presents.

Representation may be of any quality or set of qualities, e.g. occupation, geographic location, party membership (as on legislative committees in the USA, or West Germany), sex (as with one section of the Labour Party National Executive, or American National Committees), etc. 'Functional' representation is based on the choice of representatives by certain predetermined economic, social and cultural groups. 'Virtual' representation is the notion that the duty of members of a national legislature is to represent all sections of the community, even those areas or sections lacking their own specific representatives (the term was used in the arguments over the reform of the franchise in Britain before 1832).

☛ CONSTITUENCY; DELEGATION; DEMOCRACY

Republic

A form of government in which the head of state is not selected on a hereditary basis, but is elected or appointed, often directly or indirectly through the choice of the citizens or their representatives. However, there is no necessary implication that the form of government of a republic will be democratic.

Republicanism is an ideological belief that favours the abolition of some specified monarchy.

Response

Reaction to a stimulus. In political analysis, the term is used in two particular contexts: in systems analysis, response is the reaction made by components of the system to critical levels of stress, communicated to these components by feedback mechanisms; in survey analysis, a response is a reply to a question, or, in aggregate, to a complete questionnaire. In this latter context, the response rate is the percentage of people interviewed who gave a usable reply to a question or questionnaire.

☛ FEEDBACK; STRESS; SURVEY; SYSTEMS ANALYSIS

Responsibility

An obligation, by the holder of an office or other position of political power, to account for the proper exercise of his duties and powers to some superior person or group. This obligation may rest on custom, on law, or on constitutional foundations.

Examples of its operation include the doctrine of collective responsibility of ministers of the British Government to Parliament; the individual responsibility of British ministers for the actions of their civil servants; the general responsibility in representative democracies of legislators to their electors; the responsibility of administrators in certain European states to administrative courts for the legality of their decisions and actions.

A distinction is often made between arbitrary regimes (e.g. autocracies or dictatorships) and responsible regimes (e.g. parliamentary democracies or constitutional aristocracies). It is important not to equate responsible government with democratic government, though, by definition, all democracies would contain provisions for political responsibility.

Revolution

In its political usage, a relatively sudden, violent and illegal attempt to change the regime of a state or other political organisation, and in which large sections of the population are involved as participants.

It is distinguishable from a civil war, in which large sections of the population are involved on both sides, though it may be the cause or the effect of such a war (e.g. the American and Russian (1917) examples). It is more broadly based than a coup d'état or a putsch, which in any case may be aimed at only bringing about a change in the personnel of government, and not a change in the system of government.

☛ CIVIL WAR; COUP D'ÉTAT; INSURRECTION; PALACE REVOLUTION; PUTSCH; REBELLION

Role

A set of expected and repeated patterns of behaviour and clusters of attitudes associated with the fulfilment of some social function within the context of a social group. These roles are acquired by individuals through socialisation.

Political roles are thus the regular behaviour patterns and attitude clusters associated with political functions in the context of political groups, e.g. party leader, President, revolutionary agitator, 'city boss', conciliator in an international conflict. While the behaviour in such roles may be in part determined by rules, custom, tradition, etc., much of it remains discretionary; however, should actual behaviour exceed the particular bounds of discretion permitted, the individual is regarded as behaving 'out of role', and may expect the operation of social or political sanctions against such behaviour.

☛ ATTITUDES; POLITICAL BEHAVIOUR

Roll-call analysis

The analysis of opinions, attitudes or other attributes of e.g. legislators, judges, committee members, by employment of data concerning their voting record on a series of issues. This data may be analysed with the purpose of establishing and measuring a set of underlying factors; it may permit the construction of indices of party regularity; it may be used for attitude scaling, etc.

☛ ATTITUDE SCALING

Rule

As a noun, a rule is a prescription for the guidance of action, supported by sanctions. Thus laws, regulations, political decrees and, in some cases, procedural conventions may all be considered as rules.

As a verb, 'to rule' is to exercise political authority, and is thus synonymous with the verb 'to govern'.

☛ NORM

Rule of law

A normative concept, implying that government should not be arbitrary, but should be conducted through procedures authorised by legislation passed in proper form; that official status should not protect a person from the operation of normal legal sanctions, if he has broken the law; and that the rights and obligations of citizens should be laid down in the form of law, and these laws should be available for perusal.

It is particularly associated with the writings of the English jurist, A. V. Dicey (1835–1922). Though essential to democratic, or any form of constitutional, government, the rule of law is not in itself sufficient to establish or maintain democratic rule.

☛ CONSTITUTIONALISM; DEMOCRACY; DUE PROCESS

Ruling class

☞ ELITE

S

Salience

A quality of obvious prominence; thus, in conflict and bargaining theory, a solution or resolution of conflict that is clearly distinguishable by both parties from other possible solutions, though it need bear no relation to equity (e.g. a 50–50 division, the existence of a river dividing disputed territory, the existence of a line of latitude as the basis for an armistice settlement).

☛ BARGAINING THEORY; CONFLICT APPROACH

Sample

A fraction of some collectivity, known as the 'population', selected in some manner so that it can be taken to represent certain required characteristics of the collectivity, within acceptable degrees of probability.

The size of the sample relative to total population affects the degree of probability with which the results obtained from the sample may be assumed to hold for the total population, and the design of the sampling procedure is also of great importance.

In survey research random samples are used most extensively, as it is possible in this way to assess the probability of the results obtained being representative for the whole population. These random samples are obtained by using some randomising device (e.g. books of random numbers). They may be drawn directly from the population or drawn in several stages (e.g. a sample of wards drawn from a sample of constituencies). This latter practice is called 'multi-stage sampling'.

☛ STATISTICAL ANALYSIS; SURVEY

Scenario

A description of a hypothetical sequence of events, in order to focus attention on the causes of such events, and on the opportunities for critical decisions involved at various stages of the sequence. It is used to consider the way in which a series of events occurs, and alternative consequences which might have occurred if certain key decisions had been taken differently.

It can be applied to a past occurrence (e.g. the causes of the First World War), a current situation, or to possible future events (e.g. a Chinese invasion of India). Though used most generally in international politics, it can be applied to the analysis of most types of problem, international, foreign or domestic, of interest to the political scientist, and can be used in conjunction with simulation and gaming techniques.

☛ CASE STUDY METHOD; GAMING; PREDICTION; SIMULATION

Scientific method

What is sometimes termed scientific method is in fact a set of procedural rules, cautions and practices for the elimination of as much bias and error from scientific analysis and investigation as possible.

In investigation and analysis it involves the establishment of a programme or schedule of procedures; generally a working hypothesis concerning the relationship under investigation that is to be tested; the identification of variables; the careful design of an experiment or other investigatory method; the confirmation or refutation of the initial hypothesis; the development of laws and theories on the basis of verified hypotheses; the replication and verification of the initial investigation; etc.

Scientific method is thus based on logical concepts, and as such is capable, at least in principle, of application to the explanation of phenomena in the physical, natural and social sciences.

☛ BEHAVIOURAL APPROACH; POLITICAL SCIENCE

Secession

The act of separation from an existing state by some section of the inhabitants of that state, based on an identifiable territory which they occupy, in an attempt to set up their own autonomous state, or perhaps to join with some neighbouring state. Secession often occurs in federal states, being based on the supposed rights of the secessionist province to withdraw from the federation, or their claims that the nature of the federation has become disadvantageous to them in some way.

Examples of secessionist attempts: the confederate southern states from the USA, 1860–61; Biafra from Nigeria, 1967; Singapore from Malaysia, 1965.

☛ FEDERATION; SEPARATISM

Second ballot system

A system for the election of members to a legislature (or similar body), involving the possibility of two ballots separated in time, on the basis of single-member constituencies.

Though the detailed arrangements will vary from system to system, basically the method of election involves a first ballot, in which any candidate securing over half the votes cast in his constituency is declared the winner; if no candidate secures such a majority, a second ballot is held at a later date, possibly with nominations restricted to the two or three most successful of the candidates on the first ballot, and a simple plurality suffices to elect. The interval between the ballots allows time for electoral bargains to be arranged.

France uses this system for elections to the National Assembly, and it is used by the Conservative party in the British Parliament to elect its leader.

☛ ELECTORAL SYSTEM; EXHAUSTIVE BALLOT

Secondary group

A group characterised by the sporadic and impersonal nature of the interaction and intercommunication of its members, and by the instrumental nature of the purposes for which the members believe the group exists. Members are usually involved only with regard to some specialised role, of a professional, economic or political nature, for instance. Secondary groups are usually larger in size than primary groups. A political party branch, a general meeting of the shareholders of a company, a legislative committee are all examples of secondary groups.

☛ PRIMARY GROUP

Secret ballot

☞ BALLOT

Sedition

Acts which, while not falling within legal definitions of treason, are regarded by the judicial authorities of the state as likely to promote discontent or incite rebellion against the state and its rulers.

☛ TREASON

Semantic differential

☞ ATTITUDE SCALING

Separation of powers

Based on a classificatory division of the functions of government into legislation (rule-making), administration (rule application) and adjudication (the settlement of controversies arising out of rule-making or rule application), the 'separation of powers' is the normative principle that these functions should not be entrusted to the same persons if society is to be libertarian rather than authoritarian. In such terms, the United States has a high degree of formal separation written into its constitution. In Britain, such separation is more ambiguous (ministers are generally members of Parliament; the House of Lords and the Lord Chancellor occupy judicial positions as well as having legislative or administrative roles). Dictatorships generally combine these powers, at least informally, so that they fall under the control of one man or a ruling elite.

☛ ADMINISTRATION; DICTATORSHIP; EXECUTIVE;
   JUDICIARY; LEGISLATURE

Separatism

The idea that a territorial area within a state, generally one inhabited by an ethnically distinct population, should be allowed to part from the political community to which it at the time belongs, in order to govern itself, or to be free to join some other political community with which it has ethnic or other influential ties.

Separatism is closely associated with the concept of political integration, reflecting the idea that political communities will not remain integrated if there is a lack of consensus concerning the proper identity and composition of the community, and the separatist case is often based, more or less explicitly, on the claim that separation in their particular case would be in the interests of better integrated political communities, both for the original state and for the separated state. Separatist movements this century have received considerable impetus from the ideas of national self-determination (e.g. as included in Woodrow Wilson's Fourteen Points), and anticolonialism.

Separatist movements are usually prepared to employ any strategies that might advance their cause, including electioneering, rhetoric, demonstrations, violence (including terrorism), civil war and secession.

Examples of separatist movements in the twentieth century have included Rhenish and Bavarian separatism (Germany), the Basque area (Spain), Ireland (the United Kingdom), Brittany (France), Sicily (Italy), Biafra (Nigeria) and Quebec (Canada).

☛ AUTONOMY; NATIONALISM; POLITICAL INTEGRATION; SECESSION

Side payments

A term in game theory which refers to the payments made by one player to another outside the formal structure of rewards and penalties of the game itself, e.g. as compensation for making a disadvantageous formal move in the game, as a bribe to make such a move, as a means of forming a coalition, etc. It is thus a term associated with games involving three or more players.

☛ GAME THEORY

Simulation

A technique in social science research, in which a situation is created artificially (though it may be based on an actual situation) with regard to certain key aspects, and the interactions of these aspects are investigated by proceeding with the situation, on the basis of a scenario worked out in advance. Gaming is a form of simulation, e.g. when an international crisis is simulated and 'actors' take relevant roles for the duration of the simulation.

The advent of computers has meant that simulations can be programmed for a computer, and the changes in the variables of the simulated model or system observed over time. In this way, otherwise lengthy time periods can be telescoped into a few minutes of computer time, and complex interactions can be calculated swiftly. Variables may be controlled, so that several alternative simulations can be compared. One of the best known of this type of simulation was the 'Simulmatics' project which studied factors (such as John Kennedy's religion) thought likely to affect voting behaviour in the 1960 American presidential election.

☛ COMPUTER UTILISATION; GAMING; MODEL; PREDICTION; SCENARIO; VARIABLES

Single election

☞ ELECTION

Single transferable vote system

A system of balloting in multi-member constituencies, based on the voter ranking his preferences among the available candidates as 1,2,3, ... etc., rather than simply indicating one choice by a cross or similar device.

For each constituency, a quota is set (the Droop quota is usually employed, i.e. quota = votes, divided by one more than the number of seats available, plus one vote), and votes are redistributed for candidates (a) with votes surplus to the quota— these are redistributed according to the proportions of second preferences on those candidates' first preferences; and (b) with the least number of first preferences—their votes are redistributed according to their stated second preferences. For both redistributions, the total proportions of second preferences are observed, though for surplus votes they are only redistributed to the extent of the surplus. Later preferences may be brought in as necessary, should the first redistributions fail to give sufficient candidates the required quota.

☞ DROOP QUOTA; ELECTORAL QUOTA; ELECTORAL SYSTEM

Small group politics

The study of the political process within small aggregates of not more than about twenty persons, who form primary or face-to-face groups. Such groups may be informal, or formal but with a network of informal relationships in addition to their formal procedures, rules and tasks.

Such study has focused particularly upon the interactions associated with decision-making in the group; leadership; the formation of alliances and coalitions; the working of committees; the development and articulation of group norms concerning procedures, goals, and methods of implementation; communication among members of the group; participation levels and patterns; the settlement of conflicts; the development of structures within the group itself.

Political behaviour in small groups has been studied in several ways, including the examination of reports; documentary analysis; the study of biographical material; participant observation; laboratory techniques; the analysis of decision patterns (e.g. of Supreme Court judges in the USA). Artificial, or simulated, situations may also be used for experimental study.

A review of several of the theories and methods used in the study of small group politics, and an extensive bibliography on the subject, are contained in S. Verba, *Small Groups and Political Behaviour*, Princeton University Press, 1961.

☞ GROUP BASIS OF POLITICS; MICRO-POLITICS; ORGANISATION THEORY; PARTICIPANT OBSERVATION; PRIMARY GROUP; SIMULATION

Social class

A term applied to a section of a community which possesses similar cultural patterns based on social status and the prestige associated with it, income levels, values and social power. Some authorities would add to this list a shared sense of class identity. Certainly many surveys have been conducted based on the differentiation between objective social class (as defined by occupational status, income, educational level and similar factors) and subjective class (defined by self-attribution).

Marxian theory defines social classes in terms of their relationship to the means of production, and thus relates them to economic factors alone (though these may have social and political consequences). In particular, class consciousness is therefore seen as a product of industrial society, where the economic aspects of status and power seem dominant, and leads inevitably to class conflict.

Several typologies of class may commonly be found in social science. One of the simplest is the threefold division of upper, middle and lower (or working) classes. A refinement of this divides the middle-class component into two (upper-middle and lower-middle) and the working-class into such subcategories as skilled, semiskilled and unskilled, or 'white-collar' and 'blue-collar'. Other divisions have been of an alphabetical nature, such as that used by market research or opinion research agencies, e.g. A (upper-managerial or property owner, high income); B1 (middle-managerial, moderate income); B2 (clerical or administrative, low income); C (white-collar skilled workers, moderate income); D1 (blue-collar skilled workers, moderate income); D2 (blue-collar unskilled workers, low income); E (pensioners, unemployed, etc., very low income).

☛ CASTE; SOCIO-ECONOMIC STATUS (SES); STATUS

Social structure

The social structure of a society consists of its various status positions, such as class membership, marital status, occupational positions, political offices, and the roles, expectations and relationships that hold among the occupants of these status positions, as well as the institutions within which the holders of status positions have roles.

☛ INSTITUTION; ROLE; SOCIAL CLASS; STATUS

Socialism

An ideology based on the belief that the means of production in a society should be owned and controlled by the community, that the purpose of productive enterprise should be the satisfaction of communal, rather than individual, needs, and that individual fulfilment can only be realised when communal needs have been satisfied.

Such goals imply political, as well as economic changes in a society. While Communism finds in the writings of Marx and Lenin warrant for the 'dictatorship of the proletariat', socialism is based on the achievement of a democratic political regime, and most socialists would extend democracy as a form of control into the economic sphere also.

But the working-out of more detailed aspects of socialism, in its economic, political and social forms, has encouraged the formation of several 'schools'. Among the most important have been the Utopian socialists and the communistic societies associated with e.g. Robert Owen, who attempted to invent a new and 'socialistic' form of society; the French socialists, such as Saint-Simon and Fourier, some of whom were also Utopian in orientation; Marxian socialists, based on the theoretical writings of Karl Marx, and centred around the concepts of the class struggle and historical inevitability; the Revisionists, who questioned the factual basis of some Marxist interpretation and prescription; the Fabians, who saw in gradual and non-violent reform the best road for the attainment of socialist goals; syndicalism, with its faith in direct action by the workers and its distrust of reform or parliamentary action; guild socialism, relying on democratic changes in the workplace particularly; and social democracy, the 'main stream' belief of most of the socialist and Labour parties of the western hemisphere.

The 'Socialist Internationals' were attempts to create a world-wide organisation of socialists—who, by definition, were distrustful of nationalist manifestations—to coordinate and to inform the actions of individual socialist groups. The First International (1864–76) broke up over the quarrels between Marxian socialists and anarchists; the Second International (1889–1923) was fused with the International Working Union of Socialist Parties in 1923 to form the Labour and Socialist International, which, after the Second World War, became the present Socialist International; the Third International (the Comintern) was an organisation founded by Lenin to bring about world revolution, and it was soon under the hegemony of the Russian Communist Party.

☛ COMMUNISM; FABIANISM; MARXISM; POPULISM; SYNDICALISM; UTOPIANISM

Society

Though used as an imprecise term to describe many varieties of social collectivity, most uses of the term in social science include the notions of some group of persons, occupying a defined territorial area, substantially independent of other societies, capable of self-perpetuation through reproduction, and which possesses a distinct culture and institutional structure. In its political aspect, a society is called a state.

☛ COMMUNITY; STATE

Socio-economic status (SES)

A designation of the relative status of a person within the social structure, based primarily on his characteristics of income and occupation. It is used as a category dimension for purposes of survey research, etc. It differs from social class, in that its basis is more restricted in terms of the factors it includes, and in that these factors are objective, whereas social class designations may involve subjective factors such as self-identification with a class.

☛ SOCIAL CLASS; SOCIAL STRUCTURE; STATUS

Sovereignty

By sovereignty is meant the ultimate power possessed by a person or institution in a political community, to decide on political matters (e.g. the establishment of goals, the statement of priorities, the resolution of conflict) and to enforce these decisions once made.

As a philosophic concept, it arose in the sixteenth and seventeenth centuries, as the concept of the nation-state was emerging and political conflicts over the role of the Church in civil affairs were reaching their crux. Philosophers and jurists such as Bodin, Hobbes, Blackstone and Austin were all contributors to the development of the notion.

Yet observably political communities, including states, do exist without possessing the one, single, and identifiable institution that fulfils the conditions of the definition. Federal states are, by definition, states in which the political authority of both the federal and the provincial units is limited; nor can the Constitutional or Supreme Court, charged with interpreting the 'constitutional contract' of federalism, be regarded as sovereign, for it lacks power to enforce its decisions (e.g. USA, West Germany). Even at the federal level, it is clear that the President and Congress limit the political power of each other. In Britain, even the prime minister cannot be regarded as possessing the ultimate authority envisaged in the definition. Only by a circular process of broadening the concept to equate it with the *fact* of political community itself can it be claimed that in every political community there is an ultimate source of political decision and authority.

☞ AUTHORITY; POWER; STATE

State

There are many definitions of the word 'state', based on historical, legal, functional, structural, moral and other considerations. Many of these would not be inconsistent with the following: the state is a territorial area in which a population is governed by a set of political authorities, and which successfully claims the compliance of the citizenry for its laws, and is able to secure such compliance by its monopolistic control of legitimate force.

This is an 'ideal' definition, for few, if any, actual states can be said to meet all the requirements stated. In particular, compliance is not always successfully obtained; the constraints of e.g. international politics may restrict 'the monopolistic control of legitimate force'; and in a federal state there may be two distinct sets of political authorities, each claiming compliance for their own areas of competence.

Certain important distinctions must be drawn. The state is an aspect of society, but it is not a synonym for it, as it is concerned solely with the political affairs of a society. (These affairs may, however, be wide-ranging, as in a theocracy or a totalitarian society.) A state is a political system, but not every political system is a state; some are subordinate to the state, others e.g. international systems, made up of states. Nor is it necessary to equate the state with the political arrangements of a society; the works of social anthropologists such as Lucy Mair have demonstrated the existence of 'stateless' societies, which possess political organisation but not necessarily a fixed territory, a governmental structure or the monopolistic control of force. A state must also be distinguished from a nation; while the two may coincide, it is rare indeed for even the preponderant majority of a nation to occupy the same state, while most states contain a minority of nationals other than those of the preponderant nation. Many multinational states exist (e.g. the USA, Israel, Malaysia).

Marxist notions of the 'withering away of the state' result from viewing the state as the institutionalisation of class conflict; the elimination of class conflict—either by the existence of one class only, or the elimination of classes—under this definition eliminates the purpose, and hence presumably the existence, of the state. Anarchists also base their ideology on the premise that it is possible, and desirable, to arrange social relations so as to eliminate the need for the state, seeing it as a coercive institution.

The prospect of the evolution of the nation-state into international states, or even a world-state, is held by those who see in the development of international law the best, or only, prospects of man's survival on Earth.

☛ ANARCHY; COMMUNITY; CONTRACT THEORY; FEDERATION; GOVERNMENT (A): the institution; NATION; POLITY; SOCIETY

State capitalism

☞ CAPITALISM

Statism

The belief that planning, especially economic and social planning, should be placed as far as possible in the hands of the central government authorities. Statism may be associated with political movements of a left-wing, right-wing or centrist type.

☛ COLLECTIVISM

Statistical analysis

The analysis of political phenomena by any of the techniques of statistical method may be termed statistical analysis.

Among the methods which may be of use in political analysis are: the calculation of frequency distributions; measures of central tendency, distribution and probability; sampling techniques; calculations of correlation; the employment of index numbers; the analysis of trends over time.

Statistical analysis has been used to a considerable extent in voting analysis; legislative research (e.g. through roll-call analysis); communications studies; attitude and opinion research, particularly with sampling methods; and several areas of political behaviour research involving correlation analysis.

While of considerable use in the arrangement and relating of political data, the testing of hypotheses, the revelation of correlations, etc., it must be remembered that statistical analysis depends for its utility on the initial accuracy and appropriateness of the data which is available.

☛ MATHEMATICAL ANALYSIS

Status

The position occupied by a member of a social group (e.g. a community, a family, a political party branch organisation) defined by the positions with regard to him which are occupied by members of the group, and as limited by the norms, rules and values of the group. Status thus involves e.g. formal power relationships, privilege relationships, or relationships of responsibility.

A distinction is made for some analytical purposes between *achieved* status, the result of some type of competitive situation (e.g. the nominee of a political party for a presidential election, the secretary of a trade union), and *ascribed* status, acquired—at least potentially—at birth (e.g. status in a family or tribe, membership of a caste or a ruling house).

The various levels of status may be stratified according to such considerations as the amount of prestige associated with them by members of the social group concerned.

Status is regarded by many political sociologists as an important factor influencing many forms of political behaviour, including voting, membership of political groups, attitudes towards authority, etc.

☛ ROLE; SOCIAL CLASS; SOCIO-ECONOMIC STATUS (SES)

Stereotype

A set of beliefs, concerning a group or a class of people or objects, which is based upon general simplified assumptions held, often falsely, to be true, and which ignore evidence which tends to conflict with these assumptions. Even where the set of beliefs may be accurate for some of the cases in question (e.g. of some members of an ethnic group), the tendency is to disregard the cases for which it is not true and neglect the variations that exist.

People often possess stereotypes concerning inhabitants of other regions and countries, the occupants of certain positions (e.g. civil servants), organised groups (e.g. political parties) and social processes (e.g. election campaigns) which are of potential influence on their political behaviour.

☛ ATTITUDES; IMAGE

Stress

A concept in systems approaches to political analysis, which refers to those stimuli to which a political system is subject, which, if they persist at certain levels, and if the responses of the system are inadequate to cope with them, threaten the persistence of the system.

In terms of Easton's approach, stress arises when the 'essential variables' of the system—its ability to allocate values authoritatively for the society, and its ability to obtain compliance with such allocations—are threatened by e.g. a decline in support, cleavage, an excessive volume of demands, output failure, etc. For Deutsch's communications model, similar forms of stress can be identified, e.g. insufficient communication about a system's own internal state, an inability to cope with information flows, feedback failure, etc.

☛ COMMUNICATIONS APPROACH; CRITICAL RANGE;
   FEEDBACK; SYSTEMS ANALYSIS

Structural-functional analysis

A method of analysis of social systems derived from the work of anthropologists, which examines a system in terms of the structures of which the system is composed, and the functions which those structures perform. Such analysis permits comparison of similar systems in terms of structural or functional differentiation, and allows explanations to be made of e.g. changes within systems, pathological states of systems, and systems development.

One variety of structural-functional analysis concentrates on the functional requisites of a social (or political) system. Such analysis postulates that each type of system has certain requisite functions which must be performed for the system to persist (the analogy of the human physiological system is sometimes used as illustration). If existing structures are failing to perform these functions adequately, other structures may come into existence to perform them. Such analysis involves several definitional difficulties e.g. of such terms as 'requisite' and 'persistence' or 'survival' of the system. Talcott Parsons produced one such set of requisites for social systems: adaptation to the environment; goal attainment; pattern maintenance; integration of its components.

Since a system is often composed of subsystems, a distinction may be drawn between functions that are necessary, or at least favourable, to the survival of a system, and those that are unfavourable to its survival, though they may be favourable to the survival of a subsystem. The terms 'eufunctional' (or, simply, 'functional') and 'dysfunctional' are used for such favourable and unfavourable functions. Such judgments of favourability must be preceded by empirical statements of the criteria of survival if they are not to be value judgments.

Functions which are recognised or intended by members of the system are called 'manifest functions' (e.g. the legislative functions of the House of Lords, the electoral competition of political parties); those that are unrecognised or unintended are called 'latent functions' (e.g. the ceremonial functions of the House of Lords as political symbols, or the political socialisation functions of political parties).

☞ ACTION THEORY; FUNCTION; STRUCTURE

Structure

A set of independent elements or parts which operate together in some regular manner; thus, in political systems, sets of political actors which perform functions as collectivities for the political system. Such structures include formal and informal institutions (e.g. the legislature, the head of state, interest groups and political parties) and subsystems of the political system (e.g. the communications subsystem). Structures may themselves be composed of lesser structures.

☞ FUNCTION; STRUCTURAL-FUNCTIONAL ANALYSIS

Subcommunity

A social group which is characterised by the sharing of some more specific features than those possessed by the community as a whole. A community may therefore contain many different subcommunities, and an individual may belong to several sub-communities at the same time. In the USA some writers have postulated the existence of a Negro subcommunity in large cities, for example. The members of a church in a village, or of an age set in a tribe may be termed 'subcommunities'. Such subcommunities may be relevant as political entities in a political system, by virtue of their common interests and opportunities for joint political action.

☞ COMMUNITY

Suboptimisation

A term used in the quantitative analysis of multivariate problems, when, in choosing a policy from among several alternative options available, certain factors are taken as fixed, though in actuality they may vary or be interdependent with other variable factors under examination. This enables a complex policy problem to be simplified, and often to be dealt with in sections by different departments of an administration. However, any policy selected in this way is likely to be 'suboptimum' compared to the policy that might be chosen if the full range of variables were taken into account.

☞ POLICY ANALYSIS

Support

Generally, expressions or actions indicating a favourable response to a decision, policy, action, or to the existence of a particular government or regime, or a leader in such a government or regime.

More specifically, it is one of the basic categories of inputs in the systems approach to political analysis developed by David Easton. He identifies two classes of support: *diffuse*, which is support for a government or regime given in general, and over the long term, affected by, but not directly linked with, the individual decisions or policies of that government or regime, and *specific*, which is support for some particular policy or action. Should support in either of these categories fall below certain levels, stress is imposed on the system, and the authorities must respond by taking measures likely to increase support. These measures might include, in the case of diffuse support, improved communications, changes in procedural arrangements, or a general increase in demand-satisfaction, and in the case of specific support, amendment or abandonment of the policy, improved communication about the benefits of the policy, or an alteration of its timing.

Decline in support may be indicated by e.g. election results, civil disobedience, rebellion, evasion of laws, extremist political groups being formed, emigration, etc.

☛ POLITICAL SYSTEM; STRESS; SYSTEMS ANALYSIS

Survey

A detailed investigation of selected aspects of a 'population'. (The population may consist of events or other non-human items, as well as of humans.) Since, in many surveys, constraints of cost, time and other resources, or the physical impossibility of dealing with every item, rule out exhaustive investigations, sample surveys are often used instead.

Survey analysis then uses the results of surveys to check or to formulate hypotheses, to classify, to create models, etc.

☛ PANEL STUDY; POPULATION; SAMPLE

'Swing'

'Swing' is the term used to denote the measure, in percentage terms, of the relative transfer of support from one political party to another among the electorate of a single constituency, a group of constituencies, or the country as a whole. It is stated in terms of the 'swing' to one party (or, conversely, from the other party). It is calculated by taking the percentage of the poll which one party has lost compared to the previous election, and adding it to the percentage of the poll which the other party has gained since that election, and this result is then divided by two to give the 'swing' to the second party. If both parties have lost votes (due to there being more than two parties with candidates in a constituency) then the percentage loss of the first party is subtracted from the loss of the second party, and the result divided by two. Strict comparability of results is affected by the existence of third parties and variations in the percentage turnout of voters at the two elections being compared.

☛ PSEPHOLOGY

Symbol

A sign which communicates a concept, or set of concepts, to an audience. Among the forms which might be taken by political symbols are communication signals (e.g. slogans of political parties), pictorial representations (e.g. the swastika), institutions (e.g. the coronation ceremony in Britain), acts of political participation (e.g. the speech of the party leader at an annual party convention), or official procedures (e.g. the 'State of the Union' message of the American President).

☛ IMAGE; POLITICAL COMMUNICATION

Syndicalism

An ideology, associated particularly with the French philosopher Georges Sorel (1847–1922), which holds that society should be organised as a socialist community based on unions of workers. These unions would be organised occupationally, and would administer industrial production to provide the goods desired by society in the most efficient manner possible. All necessary political functions for society would be undertaken by loose federations of these unions, on a regional, national and international basis.

Syndicalism was at its most influential in France before the First World War, in Italy about the same time, in Spain before the civil war, and in parts of Latin America.

☛ SOCIALISM

Systems analysis

Systems analysis is an approach to the analysis of political structures, institutions and processes which is derived from general systems theory. It is associated most particularly with the work of David Easton, but it is also the framework for the analytical approaches of e.g. Gabriel Almond, Talcott Parsons, Karl Deutsch, and several political scientists with interests in international politics.

The Eastonian analysis of political systems focuses on the inputs of demand and support; the conversion processes by which the authorities (in a modern state system, the government, legislature, etc.) deal with these inputs; the outputs that result; the feedback mechanisms that adjust outputs to inputs; and the way the system persists in the face of stress arising from within the system or from the environment. Should stress reach critical ranges, and persist at such levels for some length of time, changes in the authorities or even in the regime (as with a revolution, for instance) may occur. Ultimately, stress may even bring about the destruction of the system itself.

The multiplicity of demands from the population of the community are aggregated into policy proposals ('issues')—by e.g. the mass media, political parties, pressure groups—and dealt with by the system. 'Gatekeepers' of various types regulate the flow of demands, to avoid overloading the channels by which demands reach the attention of the authorities. Support for the authorities, the regime and the community itself is an important input, and should it decline (e.g. through foreign subversion, a failure of legitimacy, a mismatching of outputs to demands) this would impose stress on the system. Constraints on the operation of the system, both intrasystem (lack of political resources, inappropriate communication channels) and extrasystem (such as economic or legal constraints), exist, and it is an important function of the authorities to recognise, and adapt to, such constraints.

The action theory framework of Parsons, as well as those of other structural-functional analysts, also posits the existence of a political system in which structures carry out requisite functions for the system and are involved in exchanges with the environment. Karl Deutsch, in his approaches to the study of political communication, focuses on the channels by which communication occurs in the system, the feedback processes involved, and pathological states of communication structures and processes in terms of their effects on the political system.

The values of the systems approach to analysis are that it permits the consideration in political science of non-state political systems such as the international political system, a city, a political party branch organisation, etc.; it provides a universally applicable set of classificatory categories for the comparative analysis of diverse political units (modernised and developing polities, for instance); and it draws attention to the processes of demand conversion, feedback, exchanges between the political system and its environment, and the methods by which political systems persist in the face of internal and external stress.

☛ ACTION THEORY; ADAPTATION; AGGREGATION; COMMUNICATIONS APPROACH; CONSTRAINTS; ENVIRONMENT; FEEDBACK; PERSISTENCE; POLITICAL SYSTEM; STRESS; STRUCTURAL-FUNCTIONAL ANALYSIS

T

Technocracy

The political system which would result from the replacement of politicians by technical experts. Technocracy as a form of rule is a utopian notion, which found favour in the USA in the period of economic depression before the Second World War, and which is regarded as a, possibly dangerous, tendency in industrialised states today. It is based on the assumptions that human happiness would be furthered by improving the efficiency of government, that such efficiency would result from upgrading the role of technical experts from advisory to decisional, and in doing so replacing the non-technical politician or administrator, and that, since technical criteria would be the only ones considered in taking political decisions, most controversies would be depoliticised.

Critics of these assumptions deny their validity on grounds of impossibility (e.g. many basic controversies are concerned with ends, not just with means; technical expertise tends to be specialised, so there is still a need for coordination of information and for overall 'judgment'), and deny the aims of technocracy on grounds of desirability, since, if politics is about the settlement of values, technical decisions should not be allowed to pre-empt the processes of debate and decision over values.

☞ ARISTOCRACY

Teleological explanation

An explanation which relies on statements about the purpose or intention or final state of the phenomena under consideration, e.g. 'the acorn exists in order to grow into an oak tree'. It is thus to be distinguished from explanations which rely on statements about causes.

In social sciences, the ambiguity surrounding the word 'ends' has cast doubt on the value of teleological explanations of social phenomena, since such explanations may consider either *intended* or *achieved* ends, and these do not necessarily coincide. Functional explanations are sometimes criticised as being teleological in form, and hence ambiguous and lacking in value in that they tend to neglect causation.

Theocracy

The form of government in which the rulers (often constituting a priesthood) claim to be acting as direct agents of the authority of the Deity, and in which the religious laws are also the direct source of political obligations. A theocracy is usually an absolutist form of government, on account of the imperatives of the religious laws upon which government is based. Examples include the early Hebrew state, and Tibet before the Chinese invasion.

Theory

An integrated set of explanatory laws or generalisations, which is capable of explaining some area of knowledge in coherent and systematic form. A theory is capable of generating new hypotheses, explanations and laws, as well as integrating existing explanations and laws.

Theories may be of a variety of ranges, or levels of generality. Narrow-range and partial theories deal with fairly specific subsets of facts, and seek to explain their relationships (e.g. concerning legislative behaviour in postwar British parliamentary politics). A middle-range theory explains some more general set of facts and links a wider collection of laws or generalisations (e.g. concerning legislative behaviour generally); while a general theory seeks to account for all the range of relevant facts, hypotheses, generalisations, etc., in the area under consideration (e.g. a general theory of political action, or a theory of the political system).

Theories may be modified or refuted by testing and by experience, and new theories may incorporate old ones.

☛ GENERAL THEORY; LAW (A): scientific law;
  POLITICAL THEORY

'Third world' (the)

A term applied to the developing countries, particularly those not associated formally with the American or Communist alliance systems, and which includes many former colonies of European empires. The term draws attention to the economic difficulties of these states, and their non-committed attitude towards the eastern and western power blocs.

Totalitarianism

The term applied to any system of government which claims to control, potentially or actually, all aspects of social existence within its territory. Whereas non-totalitarian government systems allow the preservation of the distinctions between the public and the private, between the political and the non-political aspects of social life, totalitarianism recognises no such distinctions.

Such total control is claimed as stemming from the imperatives of some radical ideology, one that demands not just the primacy of the political, but absorption by politics of all other aspects of social life for the ultimate achievement of the ideology's goals. Since organisations other than the state (in symbiotic relationship to the single party which acts as symbol of the ideology and its organisational vanguard) would develop values, norms and goals not necessarily in accord with those required by the ideology of the state, and might thereby endanger acceptance of the ideology, the state or the party must act as controller, or at least as sponsor, of all organisations which it permits to exist. The size of modern states necessarily involves a modern form of technology and communications media for such totalitarian control to be exercised. The forced participation of the masses in political ceremonies is also seen as necessary to the mobilisation of their efforts in pursuit of the ideological goals of the state (e.g. the building of Communism, the racial hegemony of the German *Volk*).

Since totalitarianism is an ideal type concept, it is possible to find examples only of states that have approximated to the conditions described above, but commentators usually cite the cases of Nazi Germany and Stalinist Russia, now possibly also Communist China, as the states which have come nearest to the achievement of totalitarianism.

☛ COMMUNISM; FASCISM; IDEOLOGY; MOBILISATION

Tradition

A tradition is some institution, symbol, myth or other cultural element which is passed on from generation to generation in a community, and which is regarded by some members of that community as being valuable, and relevant to the normative pattern of the community. A political tradition is a valued element of a cultural nature considered to be of relevance to the political norms of a community, e.g. the inaugural address of a new President of the USA, ceremonies associated with the succession of a new chief in certain African tribes, the traditions surrounding the maiden speech of a British member of Parliament.

Societies are sometimes called 'traditional societies' when they continue to place preponderant emphasis on tradition as the source of their political values; modernisation consists, among other things, in the substitution, in place of tradition, of rational or ideological criteria for assessing political phenomena.

Tradition is one of the sources of legitimation of leadership put forward by Weber in his typology of leadership, in contrast to charismatic or rational-legal sources.

☛ LEADERSHIP; MODERNISATION; MYTH

Treason

The crime of attempting to achieve the overthrow of the regime of a state by illegal means, by a citizen who owes allegiance to that state, though in some states the offence is more widely defined to include the attempted murder of the monarch or head of state, or aiding the enemy of the state in time of war. It is generally considered a capital crime in those states which retain the death penalty.

☛ SEDITION

Treaty

An agreement, or the formal record of an agreement, between two or more parties representing distinguishable national entities, which concerns the future relationship of these entities towards each other, and in some cases (e.g. the treaty forbidding the spread of nuclear weapons to non-nuclear countries, signed by several major powers, of 1970) towards other parties not signatories to the treaty.

Treaties sometimes go under other names, e.g. pacts, protocols, agreements, conventions. They are major sources of international law. Among their purposes have been the settlement of boundary disputes; the creation of multinational organisations; the formal recognition of an alliance; and the terms and conditions of peace settlements. The Geneva Convention on the Red Cross, 1864, the Treaty of Versailles, 1919, and the Treaty of Rome, 1957, are all examples.

☞ INTERNATIONAL RELATIONS; PACT

Two-party system

☞ PARTY SYSTEM

Typology

A division of some totality into a set of classes, or into several such sets. A typology may be used to discover new relationships among the things so ordered, to generate hypotheses, to lead on to the development of theories, and to identify areas for investigation.

Examples of typologies employed in political science include Plato's and Aristotle's typologies of forms of rule, Marx's typology of social classes, and Weber's typology of leadership styles.

☞ CLASSIFICATION

U

Underdog effect

The idea that the publication of forecasts of the outcome of an election, especially in the form of opinion poll results, can cause an increase in support for a candidate or party which is apparently losing, especially if such loss is unexpected or only marginal; and that such an increase of support would not have occurred, or would have been less, if the forecast had not been published.

☛ BANDWAGON EFFECT

Unicameral

Possessing a single chamber; thus used to refer to legislatures that are organised on a single-chamber basis. Examples include: the state of Nebraska (USA); the Knesset of Israel; most of the Länder Parliaments of West Germany; the Parliament of Hungary; the Ontario provincial legislature; the Folketing of Denmark.

☛ BICAMERAL

Unitary state

A state in which the powers of government are concentrated in a set of central authorities, and not divided as in a federal state. The United Kingdom and France are unitary states.

☛ FEDERATION

Urban studies

The study of urban areas, their social aspects, and the process of urbanisation. It makes use of the contributions of several scientific disciplines, including geography, economics, demography, sociology, planning sciences and political science. Among the areas of interest to investigators have been the demography of urban areas, the economy of towns, urban planning in its physical and social aspects, social structure and social behaviour (including deviant behaviour, such as crime), the provision of social services, transportation problems, and the development of new towns.

Political science contributes by its interests in the study of urban government, policies towards urban areas, political behaviour in urban communities, leadership in urban areas, relations between urban, regional and national authorities, etc. It is thus an area studied by political scientists in very similar fashion to local government and community studies, though somewhat wider in scope as it is not confined to predetermined administrative boundaries, as are local government political studies.

☞ COMMUNITY STUDIES; LOCAL GOVERNMENT STUDIES; METROPOLITAN POLITICS

Utilitarianism

A philosophy, associated particularly, though not exclusively, with the works of Bentham and John Stuart Mill, which asserts that pleasure and freedom from pain are the ends to which all human action is directed; that legal and moral rules alike should, or in fact do, reflect this principle; that morality is thus based on the rule that one should seek by one's actions to maximise pleasure (for oneself and for others affected by the actions) and minimise pain.

Such a philosophy has radical consequences for the political and legal arrangements of society. It implicitly supersedes creeds or ideologies based on external standards of morality. In some interpretations, it justifies a pragmatic approach to policy and legislation. Laws based on standards other than utilitarian principles (e.g. class interest, Christian theology, 'mere tradition') must be questioned and repealed as necessary. John Stuart Mill thus attacked the legal disqualifications of women, for example, and Bentham earlier had taken a keen interest in penal reform, holding that existing penal laws did not add to 'general happiness'.

Several logical difficulties are inherent in utilitarianism. First, the question of how one is to foresee the consequences not only of the action that is planned, but all possible alternatives, in order to maximise happiness, is unanswered. The 'felicific calculus' proposed by Mill to act as a guide in ordering 'higher' and 'lower' pleasures is, in practice, uncertain and subjective: 'It is quite compatible with the principle of utility to recognise the fact that some kinds of pleasure are more desirable and more valuable than others', *Utilitarianism*. Yet his methods of distinguishing between these kinds of pleasure involve the judgment of those who have experienced 'higher' and 'lower' pleasures, and the distinction between 'pleasure' and 'satisfaction'—the latter being an attribute of animals, for instance, more easily attainable by persons of 'inferior faculties'.

In its employment of concepts of utility, various economic approaches to politics implicitly draw on utilitarian ideas.

☛ ECONOMIC APPROACHES TO POLITICS; PARETO OPTIMUM; UTILITY

Utility

A concept used in economics, and by extension in economic approaches to political analysis, which refers to the value of some commodity (goods, services, etc.), as estimated by an individual by reference to his personal scale of preferences. Marginal utility is the additional value which an individual estimates he would receive from one additional unit of a particular commodity.

The concept can be applied to 'political goods' as varied as votes, money, time, prestige, security, etc. The major problems involved are those of obtaining homogeneity in the resource under consideration (e.g. political influence), and in quantifying units of the resource for purposes of calculation.

☛ ECONOMIC APPROACHES TO POLITICS; VALUE SYSTEM; VALUES

Utopianism

A philosophy which is based on speculation concerning the social and political arrangements of the perfect society. Such speculation may be prescriptive, in the sense of advocating the attainment of such a society; or it may be reformative and analytical, serving as a theoretical or 'ideal' standard by which to judge existing social and political institutions, in much the same way as the notion of perfect competition serves the economist.

Attempts have been made from time to time to put such ideas into practice, by creating communities which would abide by the social prescriptions laid down as conducive to 'utopian existence'. The experimental communities of the Chartists under their 'Land Plan'; Owen's New Lanark and New Harmony, Indiana; Brook Farm and Ripon (Wisconsin) are examples. Among fictional utopias, Plato's *Republic* is usually regarded as the earliest, but More's *Utopia* (1516) and Aldous Huxley's *Brave New World* (1932) are other examples.

Utopianism was found in various aspects of socialism, especially in the nineteenth century, and Marx himself recognised the value of such plans, though rejecting their lack of recognition of the force of history in human affairs, and their failure to appreciate that their desired ends might require violent revolution for their realisation.

☞ SOCIALISM

V

Validation

The processes by which some statement—in the form of a theory, law, relationship, explanation, etc.—is shown to be true in a particular case within the limitations of error laid down in advance. Validation may take the form of external confirmation (e.g. when a causal explanation based on one source of evidence, such as biographical data, is confirmed by another source, such as documents from a foreign archive). It may take the form of a confirmed prediction based on a hypothesis (e.g. when a theory of electoral behaviour predicts a change in voting patterns which subsequently occurs), or a relationship based on measurements, when the carrying out of the measuring operation gives quantitative results within certain expected margins of error.

☛ HYPOTHESIS; LAW (A): scientific law; STATISTICAL ANALYSIS; THEORY; VERIFICATION

Value judgment

A statement which attaches some non-empirical value to a person or object or abstraction, and which therefore is incapable of objective refutation. The statement: 'Monarchy is a good form of government' is such a value judgment. Such statements should be distinguished from those which (*a*) attach some empirical value to something (e.g. 'half the population oppose the President's financial policy, according to an opinion poll') or (*b*) are testable guides to future conduct (e.g. 'Monarchy is a good form of government if you wish to have stable political conditions', assuming that the concepts of 'stable political conditions' and 'good form of government' can be operationalised, and are not left as value statements themselves).

☞ NORMATIVE STATEMENT; VALUES

Value system

The set of values of various types which an individual or a group possesses, and the relationships among these values. The values may be implicit, or of various levels of explicitness. They tend to be organised in a hierarchy, and values concerning matters of a more specific nature will tend to be congruent with those of a more global kind, e.g. a person favouring the retention of the hereditary element in the House of Lords will probably possess a broad underlying conservative attitude toward political institutions generally.

The nature of values, whether as basic ideology, policy goals, rules, norms, etc., and the interrelationships which form them into a system, may be observed through the conduct of individuals and groups, their explicit statements of values, their cultural symbols, literature and other art forms, institutional patterns, spoken language, etc.

☞ IDEOLOGY; 'LADDER OF VALUES'; LAW (B):
stipulative law; NORM; RULE; VALUES

Values

For political analysis, the term 'values' has two related but distinct meanings. It refers to the objects which are desired, or (for negative values) disliked by political actors, e.g. security, democracy, justice, independence, power. In this sense, definitions of politics such as Easton's 'the authoritative allocation of values for a system' draw attention to the central position of values in political processes and behaviour. The second use of the term is to refer to the criteria by which a person, group, society, etc., selects or rejects goals, means of attaining goals, procedures, norms, etc. An alternative term for such criteria, in so far as they are linked coherently, is *value system*. The identification of such values and criteria, and their effects on political behaviour, is a task for the political analyst; consideration of the coherence of values, their origins, their relationships to other aspects of social life, and, possibly, the task of prescription are the concerns of the political philosopher (see, for example, the political writings of Aristotle, Hume or Marx).

☞ NORM; POLITICAL PHILOSOPHY; VALUE JUDGMENT; VALUE SYSTEM

Variables

Elements in a relationship which are capable of variation, either quantitatively (e.g. height, age, or income in the case of individuals), or qualitatively (e.g. marital status or nationality). Elements which are not capable of changing state in the context under consideration are constants, e.g. if the height-weight ratios of women were under investigation, then height and weight would be variables, gender the constant; all three would be variables if the height-weight ratios of adults were being studied.

Variables may be classified as dependent or independent. The dependent variable is the element whose state is affected by changes in the independent variable. It might be hypothesised that, for backbench Members of Parliament, a decision to vote for or against a government motion (the dependent variable) was predictable by reference to their party affiliation (the independent variable). Intervening variables are other relevant variables which affect the direct relationship between independent and dependent variables, e.g. in the above example, size of majority at the last general election might be an intervening variable which helps to account for many of the deviant cases discovered by the initial hypothesis on testing.

☞ CORRELATION; OPERATIONALISATION; PREDICTION; SCIENTIFIC METHOD

Verification

The process of establishing or confirming that a scientific statement is true. This may be done by e.g. statistical tests, replication of experiments or observations, or comparison with other statements which are related to it (as part of a theoretical structure, for example).

☞ EXPERIMENT; SCIENTIFIC METHOD; VALIDATION

Veto

The political authority of an institution (which may be a collectivity or a person) to prevent a decision or action from obtaining the requisite legal assent.

The veto may be absolute, or qualified (i.e. it may be overruled by some stated procedure); it may be permanent, or suspensive (i.e. valid only for some stated maximum lapse of time).

Examples of veto power include: the (now unused) absolute veto of the British monarch over legislation passed by the Houses of Parliament; the suspensive veto of the House of Lords over legislation passed by the House of Commons (limited in effect to one session, under the Parliament Act 1949); the qualified veto of the US President (which may be overridden by a two-thirds vote of Congress); and the veto possessed by the permanent members of the UN Security Council to prevent action by the Organisation on other than procedural matters. An informal veto was that used, for example, by the French Government to prevent formal consideration of Britain's application to become a member of the European Economic Community. This veto had no formal basis in the laws of the Community.

☞ VETO GROUP

Veto group

Any group which has, formally or informally, obtained the power to demand that it be consulted on matters of policy which may directly affect its interests, and the ability to prohibit the pursuit of proposals which it considers harmful to those interests, is a veto group. Among such groups in modern politics have been: agrarian groups in the USA, the European Economic Community, and several European states; the military and the Catholic Church in certain Latin American republics; religious authorities in Israel.

This power may rest on any of several foundations, including the need of the government for political support from the group, the political culture and tradition of the society, the strategic position of the group in relation to scarce political, economic and social resources, etc.

☛ CONCURRENT MAJORITY; PRESSURE GROUP; VETO

Virtual representation

☞ REPRESENTATION

Voting

The process of arriving at a decision by allowing the parties to the decision to choose among competing and specified propositions; or of electing persons to fill specified offices by allowing the indication of choice by voters among the candidates for those offices. Generally the proposition or candidate with the most votes is accepted as the victor, though it may happen that an absolute, special or qualified majority is required.

Voting may be by show of hands, vocally, by written or mechanical recording or similar means. Votes may be cast secretly or openly. It is generally the case that each voter has an equal vote, but other distributions of voting power may be specified by the voting rules.

☛ ABSTENTION; BALLOT; ELECTION; MAJORITY;
   PLEBISCITE; PSEPHOLOGY; REFERENDUM; VETO

W

War

A period of armed conflict between political groups, for the purposes of the forcible achievement of the goals of at least one of the parties involved, or the prevention of the achievement of such goals. The parties involved are, or consider themselves to be, independent political units.

Legal definition of a 'state of war' varies from society to society, but is often important in determining e.g. the commencement and termination of emergency powers given to the head of state or other institution of government.

☛ CIVIL WAR; CONFLICT APPROACH

Welfare state

A state which has assumed public responsibility for the provision of basic economic and social necessities to its inhabitants.

It is mainly (though not exclusively) associated with industrialisation, as this process, while increasing the risks of poverty and injury, and raising the demand for a mobile and literate population, also diminishes the likelihood that social groups below the level of the state will be able to provide adequate social services. Its philosophic justification rests on the ideas that society as a whole is responsible for (and benefits from) the wellbeing of its members, and that the circumstances of poverty, sickness, old age, unemployment, illiteracy or disablement are not necessarily marks of individual moral failure.

One of the first states to take this path was Germany, where the foundations of the welfare state were laid by Bismarck's administration, with a programme of social insurance. In England the welfare state resulted from the legislation of the Asquith administration (1908–16), especially the National Insurance Act 1911, the Education Act 1944, and the programme, based on the 1942 Beveridge Report, of the Labour Government of 1945–51. In the USA the welfare state derived from the New Deal legislation of President Roosevelt (1933–45), and the welfare programmes of Presidents Kennedy (1961–63) and Johnson (1963–69), though many welfare programmes remain the responsibility of states or municipalities.

Generally speaking, the welfare state provides education, a minimum standard of medical service, unemployment and disability payments, old age pensions, poverty relief payments and family allowances. These services are financed by some combination of fees, payments on the 'insurance' principle, and general taxation.

X

Xenophobia

Fear or hatred of strangers, especially foreigners, and their culture. Xenophobia has had important political effects, particularly with regard to political integration of multicultural states, racial discrimination in politics, isolationist foreign policies, immigration controls, etc.

Anti-Semitism can be regarded as one form of xenophobia.

☞ ANTI-SEMITISM

Z

Zero-sum games

☞ GAME THEORY

Zionism

The Jewish movement which developed from mainly late eighteenth- and nineteenth-century beginnings, based on a desire for the re-establishment of a Jewish national state in Palestine, by means of migration of Jews to Palestine from other countries. It also involved the revival of the Jewish (Hebrew) language and a specifically Jewish culture.

Major leaders of the movement included Theodor Herzl (1860–1904) and Chaim Weizmann (1874–1952). The ideas of the Zionists, as today, were by no means acceptable to all Jews, nor was there ideological agreement even within the movement. The growth of European anti-Semitism, the Balfour Declaration (1917) and the refusal of the Palestinian Arabs to compromise over questions of Jewish immigration in the period of the British mandate provided opportunities which the Zionists exploited to win support for their aims, and their ultimate triumph came when the state of Israel was proclaimed (1948) and recognised immediately by many of the major powers.